£14

THE HIDDEN LIVES OF TAXI DRIVERS
A question of knowledge

RUTH FINNEGAN

Callender Press

Old Bletchley

Milton Keynes

United Kingdom

ISBN 978-1-73989-376-7

First Edition   2022

www.callenderpress.co.uk

Callender Press

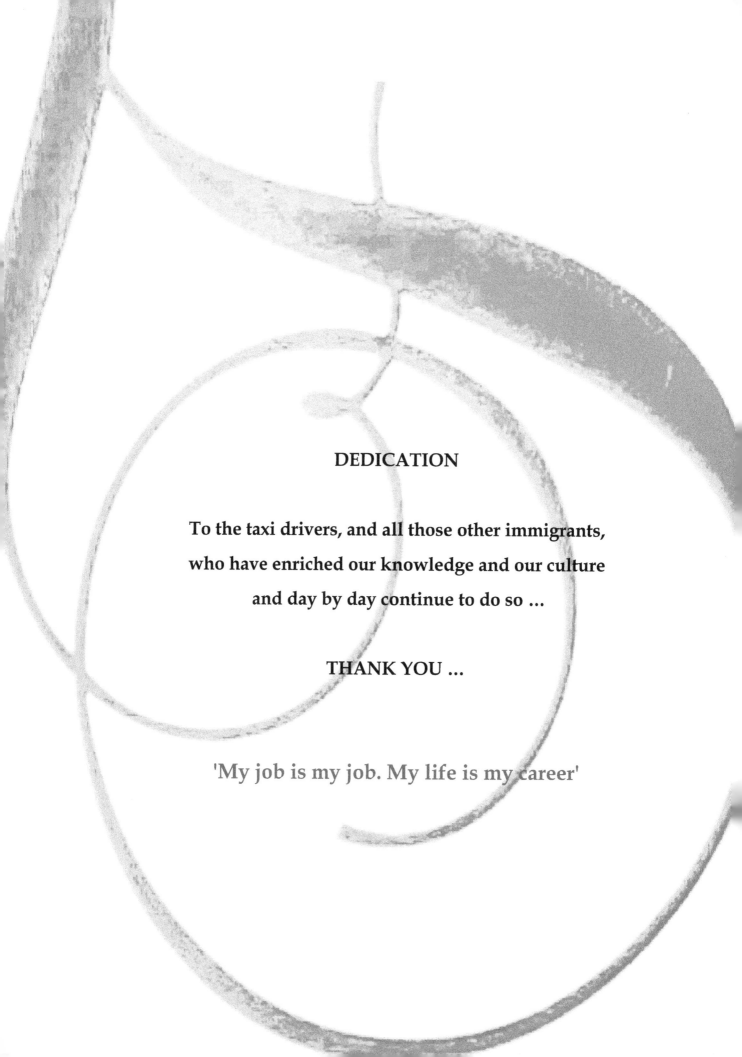

DEDICATION

To the taxi drivers, and all those other immigrants,
who have enriched our knowledge and our culture
and day by day continue to do so ...

THANK YOU ...

'My job is my job. My life is my career'

CONTENTS

KNOWING AND BEING

THERE

Milton Keynes

The Red Balloon on the image opposite, came to prominence in the 1984 BBC television advert that promoted Milton Keynes as 'a great place to live'. It featured a young boy as he travels throughout the new city of Milton Keynes with a red helium balloon. A new version was made in 2018 by local filmmaker and website designer Richard Bateman, which includes a cameo from his daughter Halle. It's a homage to the original advert but features breathtaking new scenes from around MK. The roller-skating boy is replaced by six influential local women.

The red ballon has become an icon in Milton Keynes for the success and growth of the City.

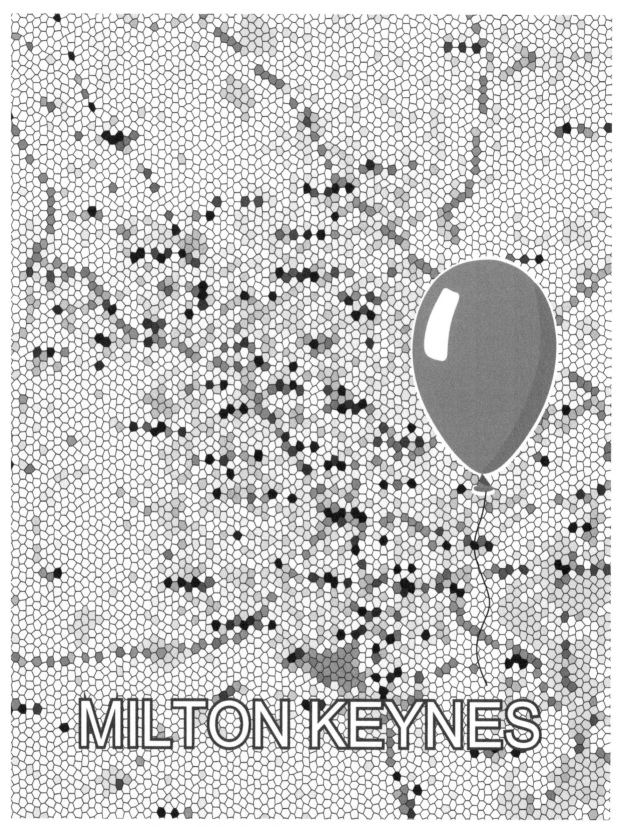

MILTON KEYNES

Designed by John Hunt, © 2022. © OpenStreet Map contributors.

Preface

Like many of my generation, I grew up thinking that using taxis was self-indulgent and unnecessary and certainly not for me. I've changed my mind. When I stopped driving in my 70s I couldn't really expect my husband to drive me all over the place. So I saw that I would have to engage taxis to go to the shopping centre or the doctor or the dentist or wherever.

So I started, at first reluctantly, to take taxis. Being a chatty person my habit was to sit in the front beside the driver. We found we were exchangIng our life stories, as far as that was possible, that is, in the typically 20-30 minute rides. And theirs were fascinating, varied, surprising.

As a result, I kind of fell into taking note by accident and then was hooked! So this study, like so many (and, come to think of it, some of my previous ones too), came about by chance. But chance is a fine thing for it turned out to link in remarkably with my earlier research interests. Like many anthropologists, I have always, I suppose, been intrigued by things that were somehow just 'there', but that I, and perhaps others too, actually knew little about in any depth. In this case it was something literally going on all around me, here on the streets, right before my eyes.

And then I saw that the here-and-now familiarity but at the same time seeming invisibility of taxi drivers – *hidden in plain sight* – chimed in with my continuing interest in the extraordinary and notable in the apparent 'ordinary' and unnoticed. For me this had in the past extended to trying to delve into the not-then-fully-studied topics of oral literature, extra-university researchers, amateur musicians, non-sensory communication, or the significance of personal names. Taxi drivers' lives were just another instance.

So I started to pay more attention to the fact that, at first without deliberately planning it, I was in practice amassing a substantial amount of information about taxi drivers. When I got a taxi whether by phoning from my own home or picking one up from the station rank or elsewhere, I would, as I say, automatically and without thinking fall into conversation with the driver. Looking back I can see this was actually a kind of informal interviewing supplementing my general offhand observating[1].

This new – to me – topic had many surprises in store. I hadn't realised how much there was that I didn't know. It also, luckily for me, turned out, as I say, to follow on well from my interest in life stories, explored among other places in my Tales of the City, and in the local informal economy and culture as in The Hidden Musicians.

I had also been fascinated from away back by memory and modes of thinking. Taxi drivers' acquisition and retention of knowledge – both remembering all the local roads, and learning of and from their passengers – proved to fit exactly with that interest. But this time it was not about something far away or long ago as many of the previous studies had been, but from people that I was meeting here and now.

And then, beyond that, I started to see taxis and taxi driving in longer perspective. There was for example the long development of hired transport which goes a fair way to explain the design and practices of modern taxis. Taxi driving in its various forms – hired transport – has,

---

[1] For a more considered account of the sources and methods for this study, see Appendix 1.

it seems, long played a crucial if largely unexplored role in the local economy of British towns (elsewhere too), interacting, for example, with transport networks, work practices, life stories, immigration, and social mobility – a pivot, in fact, in much of the social, cultural and economic history of urban space. Here were yet further dimensions to explore. All of these aspects, and more, also built into my long interests in, among other things, African studies, classical and mediaeval history, personal knowledge, and the mind. Besides I love working on an in-depth ethnography, especially one in which detail can be explored both in its own right and in wider perspective.

In this case the ethnographic setting was my home city of Milton Keynes in south central England. I had the advantage that as a long established local resident I already had substantial local knowledge to build on. In addition I had already engaged in some investigation of certain aspects of Milton Keynes' lives (Finnegan 1989/2007, 1998/2021). So it greatly pleases me to find that, unexpected by me, the present study will now be the third volume of an ethnographic trilogy about this beautiful green city of Milton Keynes, focusing down, as anthropologists sometimes do, on where I already am.

The book that has resulted, to give a brief overview gives an account of taxi driving and its organisation in Milton Keynes with special reference to taxi drivers' lives and stories and the cultural, economic and personal contexts in which they work. I have also included a modicum of parallel evidence from other UK cities such as Belfast, Birmingham, and Cambridge, and, to introduce an international dimension, the results of a few short forays abroad including several weeks' research in Auckland, New Zealand.

It also looks at some rather seldom considered aspects of taxi drivers' experience. In particular I have tried to explore their interaction with passengers in the, as it were, quasi-magical intimate space during their short, shared, journeys. And then there is the surprisingly rich symbolic lore associated with taxis, taxi journeys, and their drivers; their immigrant status; their names; their dreams; and finally of who – unique individuals within what we often see as just a general category of 'taxi drivers' – they, ultimately, are: as one put it, their 'real' selves.

All in all when I got into it I found myself wondering why I hadn't before considered – why no one seemed to have considered – taking a detailed look at the intriguing subject of taxi drivers' lives: often regarded as in a way 'the common man', yet each fully unique, individual. I embarked on it without question. Well, as I say, I just found I was in it.

I had no idea, though, what a long and demanding and at the same time enjoyable pursuit it would turn out to be. I hope that you too may find it of some interest and that the remarkable taxi drivers who participated will find it a worthy attempt to chart some of their many and diverse experiences and the settings in which they operate.

RF, Bletchley, October 2022

HERE

Chapter 1: Hidden in plain sight

*This walking business is overrated: I mastered
the art of doing it when I was quite small,
and in any case, what are taxis for?*
(Christopher Hitchens)

When, like others, I need a taxi I assume there
will be one out there somewhere, available
through the phone, the Internet, outside the
station, on the streets – somewhere. No
problem, no need to know the background –
one will just be there waiting for me.

Oh, and, I suppose, its driver too. No need to
think about *that*. Just part of the necessary
equipment. Just a taxi driver.

And then, when, as I've described, I got
interested, I started noticing how often I saw
taxis driving round, part of a line of moving
vehicles, or in traffic jams. They seemed to
crop up all over the place (except of course, as
with buses, just when you wanted one). Since
there are around a thousand licensed taxis in
my home town, their visible presence Is
scarcely surprising. But they were there not
just in Milton Keynes – there are *thousands* of
them in London for example. It was pretty
much the same in every town I've visited,
overseas as well as in England.

Here, there, and everywhere

Yes, taxis are everywhere, a necessary and
expected adjunct, it seems, of urban life.

In London above all thousands of black cabs
throng the streets (24,000 of them it is said,
and 40,000 minicab drivers) and have featured
in just about every fictional account set there –
how could you describe London without the
famous black cabs and their incredibly
knowledgeable drivers?

Or get around without a taxi in Cambridge or
Brighton where there's just about nowhere
you can park your car? In Glasgow or
Birmingham or Belfast, whether at airport or

train station or street corner – get a taxi and
rely on the driver to know the way to your
destination. The same abroad – Auckland,
Austin, Milan, Moscow, New York, wherever.

The acquired street knowledge of taxi drivers
is famous. So when I or others don't know
how to get to our destination and need to be
sure of getting there, and in time – it's a taxi,
what else?

So – they are everywhere

And – invisible

Everywhere – but somehow not there, not
noticed. Both the vehicles themselves and,
even more, the drivers seated quasi-invisible
within them, are seen only when needed. They
can be for granted as a kind of automatic part
of the service – certainly not individuals with
their interests, their joys and sorrows, their
lives in the past and present.

This relative invisibility of these near
ubiquitous taxis and their drivers is at first
sight deeply puzzling. How can we be so un-
noticing and uncurious about the experiences
and characteristics of fellow human beings?

In fact this is exactly the kind of 'invisibility'
that happens when something is too familiar
and, as it were, 'natural' for us to pay attention
to it, far less think it calls for academic study.

There – but only <u>really</u> there when you are looking and need one

For many years this was the case with other 'obvious' subjects: with notoriously 'invisible' housework; with amateur artists and craftspeop'grey' economy. Despite some laudatory attempts, it is still largely so with the artistry of ordinary speech, non-sensory communication, or the everyday arts of room decoration – indeed with the many aspects of ordinary living that we just take for granted. It is only relatively recently, for example, that 'everyday life' or 'street culture' have become accepted objects of research.

These 'hidden' arts are, it is true, sometimes captured and studied – often wonderfully – by the discipline of folklore, especially in North America and Scandinavia. But, in Britain at least, they less often gain recognition as subjects for 'serious' scholarly research.

This is certainly so of taxi drivers, for all their ubiquity. *Everywhere* – and yet when, as a typical academic, I looked for the 'literature' on taxis and taxi drivers – serious research-based writing that is – I could find next to nothing. I have been on the look-out for years. Even the massive *Sage Handbook on Transport* has, amazingly, nothing in its index for taxis, cabs, or hired vehicles, let alone any account of the drivers.

It is true that there are some excellent single-issue treatments, such as Gambetta and Hamill's analysis (2005) of 'trust' among taxi drivers in New York and Belfast, a chapter in Danny Miller's pioneering study of car-driving (2004), Mathew's notable account (2005) of political action among New York's taxi drivers, a few insightful if scattered articles (such as Anon 2014 and Thrift 2001), and a certain amount of so-called 'grey literature' in personal memoirs and diaries like Jack Clyde's often hilarious but perfectly believable memories of his encounters with his passengers (Clyde 2004) and others listed in the Select References at the end of this book[2].

It is true too that in some ways it is a popular subject, not only in personal memoirs but also in film, television, childrens' books, and a host of colouring books and so on[3], books of humour (often very funny) and taxi sayings, and a plethora of well-selling accounting notebooks for drivers.

Taxis, with their quasi-invisible and unseen, unseeing, drivers also enter as emotionally laden settings for the start of an adventure or a love affair in novels. They come in our verbal idioms, they enter into our symbolism, they are good for puns and jokes – like the 'hail a cab', contemptuously used of an unskillful jockey throwing up one arm to try to stop falling off; of a political opponent being told to 'taxi' himself off. In the U.S. 'taxi' is a slang way to refer to a prison sentence of between five and fifteen years (an analogy between a short taxi ride and a prison term?). And everyone is intrigued and astounded by the London black cabbies 'knowledge'.

But taxi drivers' *lives* seem to be almost totally undocumented in any general or analytic way. There seem to be no systematic attempts to document the general patterns of their backgrounds; about how they come to be where they are; how, for good or bad, their work is organised; their beliefs, choices, ambitions and dreams; their education and learning. Above all and most elusive of all, questions about *who*, uniquely, each one essentially *is*.

All in all, as I learned more and more about the fascinating subject of taxi drivers' lives, I was increasingly taken aback that the *human* dimensions of such an important sector of the

Everyone knows about the ways of taxis and their passengers so this jokey hotel napkin always vastly amuses (courtesy, The Vincent Hotel, Southport)

local culture of our towns today remains so largely unresearched[4].

This book is an attempt, however incomplete, to do something towards filling that gap and leading to some greater understanding and, indeed, appreciation, of a remarkable segment of our life today.

Dear Vincent Cab Driver

Please take me home to:

Address

Look for my cash in

- [ ] my bag
- [ ] my top
- [ ] my bra
- [ ] other
- [ ] my trousers
- [ ] my skirt
- [ ] my boxer shorts
- [ ] my shirt
- [ ] my socks
- [ ] my thong

Thank you

Chapter 2: The history that created taxis

Where did taxis come from? and who invented them? A look at the history of hired transport helps us understand the vehicles and practices of taxis and taxi driving today. Looking at this long back history puts today's taxicabs in clearer perspective and to a large extent explains how the form they now take is the result of long and gradual development over centuries.

Further, though taxi services may now typically be provided by automobiles, in other places and times a series of other carriers or vehicles have been in play. There have been litters, rickshaws and pedicabs, as well as animal-powered vehicles, such as hansom cabs, or boats like water taxis or Venetian gondolas, all in their setting taken for granted as *the* way for their hirers to travel.

To start at the beginning: humans (well, those who could afford it, and some who perhaps couldn't) have always been prepared to purchase transport. But the forms this transporting has taken have been varied in the extreme.

Feet and hooves for hire

It began away back, no doubt, with someone walking with another human on his (probably his maybe her) back. It must have started with members of your own family but then as inequalities emerged some people started to be able to *pay* for someone to carry you. For many centuries that must have been the commonest of hired transport, the historic equivalent of modern taxis.

It is easier of course when more than one pair of feet and hands can share the load. So we come to litters.

Hindu priest in a human drawn taxi

---

2 Such as Findlay 2010, Garner and Stokoe 2000, Lee 2012, Lockett 2017, Parry and Pye 2012, Salomon 2913, also further examples at www.taxidrivers memoirs.Many more at www.amazon.com/.

3 It is possible of course that hitherto unseen research on taxi drivers' is lurking somewhere in the woodwork and, hopefully, may emerge as a result of the present volume so as to expand and/or query its findings.

4 On the links of this study to and from other research topics see Appendix 3.

Wealthy houses in the ancient and mediaeval world had their own litters and slaves or servants to carry them, but some hired others to do the work for a fee in money or kind, or in a return of favours. Royal litters, from wherever obtained or borrowed, were full of pomp and show – a political gesture as well as for practicality. Those in the Middle East were perfect, curtained, vehicles for the transport and concealing of hidden feminine charms. And then there was the magnificence of litter travel in China.

Four footed beasts too have long played an important part. Throughout history people have utilised a wide range of domesticated animals for this purpose, among them donkeys, llamas, horses, mules, camels, dogs, elephants, and for leisure purposes as well as for serious, sometimes very long, journeys.

Great lords and royal courts could afford to own their transport but of course not all travellers could manage that, one wonders for instance, if the 'three wise men' personall owned the camels we regularly see them riding. But they could be borrowed ('hired', that is) for a price, either just the animal(s) or also someone to lead, ride or drive them – the forerunners of the taxi drivers of today. All this could at one point – indeed in some places does still – amount to organised transport for a price, whether as ridden, beasts of burden or draught animals, sometimes with their own drivers, like the elephant's mahout, sometimes (unlike in taxis) with the passengers themselves doubling in that role.

And then there was the amazingly effective and long continued post-house system of rented horses. This went back millennia to the Roman and Persian system of thousands of stations throughout their empires providing relays of horses and carriages, the antecedent of the standard transport system in England in the Middle Ages and after. In this system, a traveller could find a 'post house' every few hours along the main routes where, either driving himself, using his own drivers, or taking advantage of a post house postilion, he could exchange his horse or horses for another, fresh, animal, to take him to the next stage, then a further exchange – and so on through the length and breadth of the country. It was a competitive business.

Vector Open Stock vectoropenstock.com

Many settlements had two competing post houses, like for example the Cock and Bull coaching inns (famous for the fabulous unbelievable stories travellers would exchange there) on the same side of the main north-south route in Stony Stratford (they are still there as modern day pub and cafe). Their fierce rivalry took the firm of promising better horses (they inevitably varied), speed of harnessing the new team, facilities for rest and food if the travellers so wished, or the stable boys running out to hand up free refreshments while the new team was got ready in minutes.

All in all it was a remarkably efficient and sustained interlocking system, and travellers could set out on even the longest journey confident of being able to hire teams on the way to get them to their destination.

Boats for hire

It may at first sight seem strange to think of hired transport as not a vehicle on wheels, but a boat or ship. But for centuries water provided the main thoroughfare for travel and the vehicles for transporting people and goods were ships. And ships, like other means of transport, could be hired. The author of the famous hymn 'Amazing Grace', for example, was not only the captain of a slave-carrying ship before his conversion, but had earlier himself been captured and held as a slave in Nigeria.

The Cock and Bull Inns in Stony Stratford High Street, Milton Keynes. The High Street (commonly known as the Watling Street) – is a major 'Roman' road in England and Wales. It runs for about 252 miles (406 km) from London to the Irish Sea at the ferry port of Holyhead

Amazing as it may now sound, his father had hired a ship with its captain and crew to rescue him. There were many other cases too, almost (provided you had the money) an off-hand and taken for granted way of transporting people and goods. And of course sea transport continues. Now as for centuries past the sea and waterways are routes for travel and goods. Sometimes it is hired transport for cargo (something taxis too are sometimes employed for), sometimes it is passengers sharing the cost – another kind of hiring: dividing up the expense of hiring, as in trains and buses today.

Inland waterways too have always been favoured thoroughfares whether for necessary travel, commerce, or pleasure. London water taxis still ply a good business, and water holidays on rivers and canals, often with a boatman in charge, are still popular – a waterborne species of taxis after all – facilitated by a complex network of locks and lock keepers and, like land taxis, subject to inspection for safety.

n board a river water 'taxi' from Putney in West London h the city centre and go to Canary Wharf and Woolwich, really quite quicvklyl

Wheels, wheels, wheels

And then there are the multifarious ways that *wheels* are utilised to carry people. It can be wheels propelled by two or four feet on *pedals*, a common device in the east in the form of the rickshaw, a sort of human-powered taxi, dating from 1887 onwards[6]. These vehicles were principally made for public hire rather than private use and are still plentiful on eastern streets, especially in the Indian subcontinent. Some are dilapidated and falling to bits but others are beautifully decorated works of art. Like the hackney cabs of today, their drivers hang around the streets and at likely gathering places offering their transport. Like modern taxis too they compete for their fares and – again the same – must know the routes.

And then of course there are animal-drawn vehicles for hire, like the ox-carts, long a popular form of hired family transport in Asia, for visiting missionaries or functionaries as for locals. These often had their own expert drivers who as with modern taxi drivers, might or might not own the vehicles they drove.

In the west the post house system made travelling with hired teams a taken for granted mode of hired transport across all parts of the land.

Hand painted Bangladeshi rickshaw and driver
(Lahiri-Dutt and Williams 2010)

---

6 Rickshaw: from jinrikisha, a word popularised by Rudyard Kipling, coming, appropriately, from the Japanese jin, 'a man', plus riki, 'power' and sha, 'carriage'.

17th century hackney coaches (Gilbey 1903)

Hackney carriages and all

And yes – this leads us into the background of modern taxis. The term 'hackney' originates from the name Hackney, a once rural village, now part of London, and a good place for keeping horses. The term gradually evolved to mean, first, good horses for riding or driving; then horses for hire; then, in time, horses for drawing carriages; and then, eventually, the hired vehicles themselves. From the early seventeenth century these carriages were around in large numbers on city streets, typically four-wheeled vehicles drawn by two horses and carrying up to six passengers.

These carriages for hire were to be found everywhere in urban streets in the seventeenth to nineteenth centuries, and became a stock motif almost any novel portraying that time. In Georgette Heyer's popular and fully researched Regency novels for example, they are there to get a hero or heroine into the next stage of some adventure. They were always, it seems, easy to find, the only issue being to choose the least unprepossessing of the several clamouring jarveys (drivers) on offer.

The first documented public hackney coach service for hire was in London as early (it's hard now to believe!) as 1605. By 1625 carriages were available from London

Fiacre, 1853 (Publisher Encyclopædia Britannica)

innkeepers for hire to merchants and visitors, with the first hackney rank outside the Maypole Inn in the Strand in 1636.

A similar service was started by Nicolas Sauvage in Paris in 1637 with vehicles known as fiacres[7]. The first fiacres were boxlike, four-wheeled, open, hooded vehicles that were drawn by two or three horses and were designed to navigate the muddy Parisian streets. In 1794 about 800 were in use in Paris, and by the 19th century there were more than 1,500.

Like later taxi cabs and other money-making activities, the carriages were regulated and, in time, taxed by government. 'The Hackney Carriage Act' to legalise horse-drawn carriages for hire was passed by the English parliament in 1635. A further 'Ordinance for the Regulation of Hackney-Coachmen in London and the places adjacent' was approved in 1654 and the first hackney-carriage licences issued in 1662, their numbers in any one area subject to control. Here was the government, as ever, taking a legal and financial interest in any important, taxable and potentially disruptive activity.

A newer version was patented in 1834 by Joseph Hansom, an architect from York. This was a substantial improvement on the older vehicles for these two-wheel carriages were fast, light enough to be pulled by a single horse (cheaper therefore than the four-wheel coach), and more agile in crowded streets as they had a low centre of gravity for easy cornering. The form was later modified by John Chapman and others but retained Hansom's name. It is interesting incidentally to see the shape of these horse-drawn carriages, with their influence not only on the later motor-powered taxis but also on rickshaws. As with the comparable continuities between the stage coach (in which passengers hired individual places), and modern buses, history seems to progress less by leaps and bounds than by a gradual morphing of forms and processes.

These newer hansom cabs soon spread to other cities in Britain and Europe. They were particularly popular in London, Paris, Berlin, and St Petersburg. Then they were taken up in the late nineteenth century in other British Empire cities and the United States, especially New York. So, from this, we come to 'modern' taxis.

---

[7] The name was because the depot was opposite a shrine to Saint Fiacre (*fiacre*, like the German *Fiaker*, is still used in French to describe a horse-drawn vehicle for hire).

20

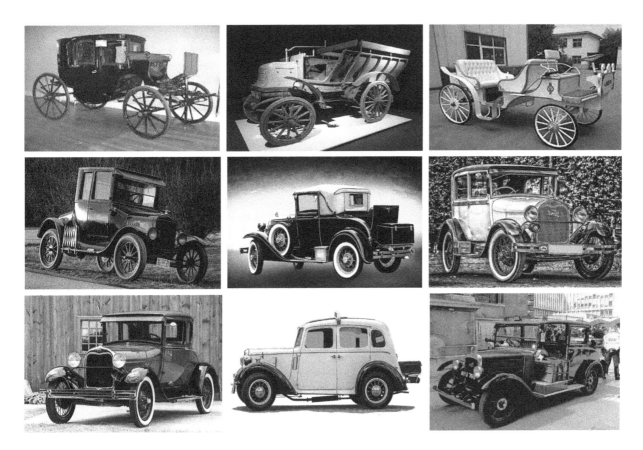

Motor taxi cabs

Modern taxis are directly linked to, and the outcome of, these earlier forms. This can be shown most vividly through a series of images followed by some further description of the intriguing processes of development. Looking at the shapes of these early motor-driven vehicles, no one can doubt their descent from the hansom cab – the gradual development and modification of existing forms. One only has to look at some of the early pictures, fruit of the equally impressive art of photography. In 1897, London became the first city to host licensed taxicabs. But as we have seen transport for hire had been around long before that. So now there is the London hackney carriage, the famous 'black cab', still with clear traces of the name and shape it came from. And then by the early 20th century taxicabs were on urban streets around the world.

Škoda Superb II Combi cab on taxi station next to the
Hämeenlinna railway station in Hämeenlinna, Finland

Miscellaneous dates of interest for London taxis (innovations later spreading elsewhere)

- Twelfth century: River barges, chiefly between royal palaces on the Thames
- Sixteenth century: Development of (horse drawn) hackney carriages for hire
- 1625: Around 20 Hackney Coaches for hire, operating largely out of inns and hotels
- 1634: London's first taxi rank, made up of four hackney carriages owned by Captain John Bailey (a member of Sir Walter Raleigh's expeditions) by the Maypole in the Strand with code of conduct for his employees – along with a special livery to mark his carriages out from others, a code of conduct for drivers with strict rules on what they could charge
- 1684: Hackney can licensing starts
- 1823: Two-wheeled 'cabriolet'/hansom cab (could be drawn by one horse)
- 1851: 'The Knowledge' tests introduced by Police Commissioner Sir Richard Mayne, following complaints about non-knowledgeable London drivers by visitors to the Great Exhibition in that year
- 1862: Act of Parliament establishing the Commissioners of Scotland Yard to regulate horse-drawn carriages within London and limiting their number to 400 (later raised)
- 1884: 1,214 drivers of horse-drawn vehicles passed 'The Knowledge' test (717 failed)
- 1891: Taximeter invented by Wilhelm Brunhild
- 1897: Battery operated cabs launched by William Bersey
- 1901: One licensed London cab (by 1991: 16,500)
- 1902: First internal combustion motor taxis
- 1907 : Taximeters compulsory
- 1939-45 war: Many taxis and drivers temporarily requisitioned by the Auxiliary Fire Service (AFS) to tow trailer pumps.
- 1948: Austin FX3 became common taxi vehicle
- 1994: Celebration of 300 years of continuous licensing (1684-1994)

- 2004: Satnavs spreading, but London black cabbies still using and tested on 'The Knowledge'.
- 2012: Uber taxis
- Now: Increasing numbers of 'green' electric and 'robotaxi' vehicles

The 'classic' Austin FX3

A major trial of driverless cars was begun on the roads of Milton Keynes in January, 2022. People were able to order a ride through an 'App'.

So-called robotaxis are popping up all over China. Tech giant Baidu, better known for its search engine and sometimes referred to as China's Google, is among the companies testing the self-driving taxi service (Aug 2022).

---

8 This is not so one sided as it might appear as it is in urban settings that by far the largest numbers of taxis are found; we should note that by now more than half of the world's population live in towns, in Britain over 80%

9 Between March 2017 and March 2022 the local council issued 1,469 licenses issued for Drivers and 156 Operator licenses (O'Driscoll 2022)

As always, then and now, there was competition among both companies and individual drivers.

WELBECK MINICAB
WELBECK 4440

One shilling per mile. No extras. Go anywhere—we lik journeys. No charge for empty Minicab's return. Waitin only 7/6d per hour. This is roughly half the price of a l taxi & for 3 people little more than the cost of pub

From a 1961 business card (Townsend 2007)

WARNING

Every year in London there are 100's of rapes and sexual assaults and 1000's of robberies committed by unlicensed minicab drivers.

Don't become a victim
only use a traditional licensed taxi

REMEMBER NO (TAXI) SIGN MEANS IT'S NOT A (TAXI)

Black cabs only!
Advert on the back of a London hackney cab receipt

It is interesting to note how, as ever, developments came about from two directions.

First it was because of changing conditions or needs: hired hackney carriages emerging when keeping a private carriage became too expensive for many owners, and taxi drivers' knowledge test being set up when the need for accurate knowledge of London was revealed during the Great Exhibition; and second, from the personal initiative and inventions of individuals, both famous and not so famous.

And on ...

Besides the gradually emergence of the present predominant version(s) of taxis, there have also been, and are still being, other developments. One thing is – what makes them go? There have been many ways in both past and present by which hired vehicles have been propelled. In modern streets it is now seldom vehicles

drawn by horses – though this still happens in some places – as there have been a number of different mechanisms over the years.

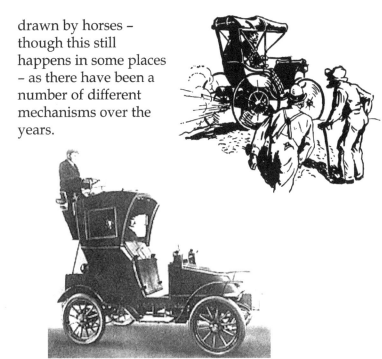

1905 Vauxhall emulating the traditional horse-drawn hansom cab (JB Collection)

When motorised taxis first got going, various fuels were tried, alternatives for horses (though we still measure by 'horse power'). Electric battery-powered taxis began appearing in the streets of London in 1897, known as 'Hummingbirds' from their sound, while in the same year in New York, the Samuel's Electric Carriage and Wagon Company began running [12] electric hansom cabs, expanding over the years.

The world's first gasoline-powered taximeter-cabs, the Daimler Victorias, started in Stuttgart in 1897, in Paris in 1899, in London

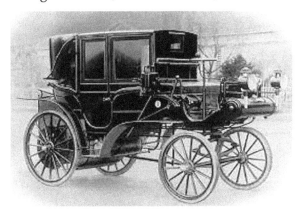

in 1903. They appeared in New York streets in 1907, then, later, in many places throughout the world where they often still operate.

Over the years many fuels have been tried for both taxis and private vehicles: electricity (starting with batteries), several different forms of petrol, diesel, vegetable matter and, as now urged by some, solar and nuclear energy. One major technical innovation came in the late 1940s, when two-way radios were first used in taxicabs. These made it possible for taxi drivers and dispatch offices to communicate and serve customers more efficiently than by the previous method of using callboxes.

Soviet GAZ M-1 taxis in 1938

The next great innovation occurred in the 1980s when computer assisted dispatching was first introduced. By now the development of computers has enabled drivers to communicate with their dispatchers through smartphones in their vehicles, or have their trips organised through web-based devices such as the Uber and Bolt Apps.

On a different tack, It is also interesting to look at the evolving language around these hired vehicles and the reasons for it. The now taken-for-granted terms 'taxi' and 'taxi cab' have an unexpected history. The name 'taxi' itself is shortened from 'taxicab', which is derived from the two words: 'taximeter' and 'cabriolet'. The term 'cabriolet', eventually shortened to 'cab', was used to refer to a one-horse carriage

with two wheels where the driver stood in the back of the carriage. The word comes from the Italian *capriolare,* 'jump in the air, capering, like a goat', so-named for the vehicles' 'light, leaping motion' (how far that might accord with modern taxis' movement I leave you to judge …)

KOSMOS TAXAMETERS

Specially adapted for OWNER DRIVERS, and for such is undoubtedly the best Taxameter on the Market.

LARGELY USED IN LONDON AND ALL PROVINCIAL TOWNS.

Special terms to OWNER DRIVERS.

Apply to . .

The Premier Taxameter Co., Ltd.,
106, ALBANY STREET, LONDON, N.W

1914 advert for a 'taxameter'
(Mann and Overton's Road Atlas, 1914)

More complicated, the word *taxi* ultimately goes back the ancient Greek word τάξις (*taxis*), which means 'payment' and was used in the French term *taximètre* (' measuring the payment'). From this the recent 'taxi' is drawn from the 'taximeter', a mechanical device invented in Germany in 1891. It was used to automatically record distances and calculate the fare, which was (and still primarily is) based on the distance travelled. From March 1898 the taxicabs in Paris were equipped with them, first called *taxibread*, then renamed *taximètres* in 1904. Then Harry Nathaniel Allen of The New York Taxicab Company, who imported the first 600 gas-powered taxicabs from France into New York in 1907, borrowed the word 'taxicab' from London, where the first documented use of the word 'taxicab' was in the March of that year.

This fitted well with the system in horse-drawn hansom cabs where the fare was paid to the driver through an opening in the back of the interior between the driver (at the back) and passenger(s) in the cab.

With meters installed pricing and payment were that much easier, and the term 'taxi'transferred from the measuring device to the vehicles equipped with them.

So now we have our taken for granted modern 'cabs' and 'taxis'. This then is the background to the modern taxi business and, necessarily, its drivers. There have been many twists and turns and changes in detail – donkeys, horses, stagecoaches, as they gradually mutated from hackney carriages into the taxicabs of today, and the cultural, economic and personal contexts in which the drivers lived and worked.

We again see the interaction of unforeseen technical developments interacting with people's needs and individuals' initiative. It might have turned out otherwise, but whatever the details, the need is constant: people want to be transported from place to place, and in practice find the resources to do so.

So it is that, here and everywhere in city streets we see transport driven for hire and, out of that gradually evolving history which explains our present system, we have today's 'taxis' and their drivers – everywhere.

Chapter 3: The urban setting and its taxi drivers

And so from all this it has come about that now, when, like many other people who do not drive and also many who do, someone wants to get a cab they can easily do so. It is in towns that taxis most visibly work and the account here will be of taxi drivers operating in an urban setting, and more particularly in Milton Keynes. Here as in other towns taxi drivers provide a much-used much-needed service and hundreds of them are licensed to travel the roads and convey passengers.

Taxi drivers in the town: how they do it

The first way a taxi driver gets a passenger is if he[10] is driving one of the cabs that, particularly in London (the 'black cabs), can be hailed anywhere. So they cruise round the streets with the taxi notice on their roof lit up to show they are free.

Their attention is attracted by would-be passengers waving, calling or whistling to them. The driver pulls up next them, perhaps (nifty drivers all) after a hair-raising u-turn in the road. The prospective passenger then either leans in the now opened front window to tell them the destination or gets straight in, helped if needed, and stretches forward from the back seat to indicate the destination. No need for detailed directions, the drivers are assumed, by some miracle of knowledge, to know the way.

There is a partition between the back and the front seats, often plastered with advertisements, so it might seem that talking though it is not possible but though passengers may have to raise their voice a little there is actually often a lot of conversation. Cabbies have the deserved reputation of being a chatty lot and full of themselves as well as interested in their passengers' stories and identities – all very enjoyable for those passengers who are sociable but also all right for the super quiet as drivers have trained themselves to be quick to pick up what is wanted. There is a small opening in the partition through which passengers will later pay the fare but also good for talking through.

A lit-up display above the windscreen shows the running total the driver will be paid, calculated on the basic pick-up charge and the mileage covered plus any specially long en route hold-up or passenger-caused wait.

---

[10] Though there are indeed some women drivers, the overwhelming majority are male and I will take the liberty of referring to drivers in the masculine gender rather than repeating the clumsy 'he or she' throughout. But please remember that in this volume 'he' should always be understood as followed wherever appropriate by 'or she'.

On arrival the driver is paid the amount on the meter by either cash or card. The passenger is expected to add a tip of around 10%, in theory optional, but in practice difficult to avoid. Then with, as conventionally expected, farewells, mutual thanks and assistance if needed, the driver opens the door (locked during transit) and drives off in search of the next fare.

The knowledgeable drivers of these roving 'black cabs' or 'hackney cabs' are famous all over the world. They are among the iconic sights and experiences of London, and used by people from every walk of life.

Second, in most cities there are approved places – 'taxi ranks' – where drivers licensed to be there congregate with their vehicles, sometimes in large numbers. Taxi ranks are typically to be found outside railway stations or other well frequented sites designated for the purpose. The drivers range themselves strictly in order of arrival, though exceptions are made if a disabled passenger or their helper hails one directly, thus allowing it to thankfully pull out of the line. Sometimes drivers have to wait for very long periods in these queues.

Drivers' particular hate is the underground one-way queue at Euston station in London where they may have wait for an hour or more in gloomy cramped surroundings, moving forward, inch by inch. It is felt worth it however as they are ready poised for the next influx of train arrivals so there will be a guaranteed fare at the end of it. But then perhaps the passenger only wants a five minute ride – back into the end of the queue again! In London the ranks are of traditional 'black cab' design, elsewhere it may be a mixture of London-like vehicles and ordinary cars of all shapes and makes. But whatever, they all keep strict order, moving up slowly till they reach the head of the queue where they find their prospective passengers waiting.

Specially, outside stations, these queues are often long, as drivers, in a fully ordered line, gradually inch their cabs forward. Finally a driver reaches the front of the queue and the passenger engages it in the same way as for the free-floating black cabs.

The third way is for drivers of taxis not licensed for either on-street pick-up or taxi-rank waiting.

Their vehicles are usually referred to, somewhat misleadingly, as 'minicabs' (some are actually as large as the black cab type) or 'private hire vehicles'. These licences, which the driver must always prominently display, are cheaper and easier for drivers to obtain than the 'hackney cab' arrangement but still an obligation: without it a driver may not legally drive a vehicle for hire.

These taxis can only be booked beforehand – pre-booked – something done not by the driver himself but by an operator, usually on the phone, speaking for the driver's sponsoring firm, who then tells the nearest driver the name, pick-up place and destination. Without this, minicab drivers are forbidden to pick up passengers.

The requirement only to take bookings in this way, beforehand, is strictly observed by drivers in fear of otherwise losing their place with the firm they are signed up with and on whom they depend for getting passengers.

For drivers, the telephone operators who take their bookings are an essential cog in the system. Highly skilled, they swiftly take the name and location for the pick-up as well as the address and postcode of the destination and tap these into the system. They know the area well, can answer prospective passengers' questions about how long the journey is likely to take, and how quickly the next available cab will get to the pick-up address. Though there are the occasional lapses, in general the system works remarkably well.

A pre-booked driver waiting for his passenger

Passengers who have booked through their mobile phone – a common method – then get a text message confirming the details, followed in due course by 'on the way' with information about the car's make, colour and number, and eventually (signalled by the driver – sometimes somewhat prematurely) 'Your taxi has arrived'; in that way the driver can avoid a lengthy wait for the passenger to appear.

The driver is then expected to proceed rapidly to the agreed destination and meet the passenger at the exact right spot.

This is sometimes no easy matter – a driver must have eagle eyes as well as fully knowing the route (plus being aware of any temporary obstacles like accidents or closed roads).

There is no viewable meter in the minicab vehicles but a set price for distance covered which the driver can check, if needed (he often knows already) from a printed list of fares. Passengers are generally happy with this but there is some room for bargaining (not that most passengers bother). The convention is for minicab drivers not to expect a tip. If asked, and, in some cases, routinely, drivers give the passenger a receipt.

Minicabs are convenient to order, normally cheaper than the hackney kind, and their drivers generally expected to be friendlier and more accessible. They are mostly just ordinary small cars but sometimes quite grand (not at all 'mini'), and generally have the name and telephone number of the firm prominently displayed on the side.

---

[11] taxi-point.co.uk/post/uber-rival-bolt-launches-in-milton-keynes/, bolt.eu/en-gb/cities/milton-keynes/

Unlike with the other two types, it is almost always possible, apart from during the covil period of lockdown, for the passenger to sit in the front seat next to the driver (this is how my study inadvertently began). Sitting side by side, conversation is easy and in most cases welcome.

This third arrangement, minicabs, is the one most commonly used by local people and traditionally has the largest number of drivers.

Added to these long-established modes in the last decade are now the drivers of vehicles for which the trips are arranged not through central operators or directly with the drivers themselves but through a web app activated by the prospective passenger. The leading players in Britain are Uber and, more recently, Bolt. Here the passengers do not have to detail their location or even know where they are as this is automatically detected through the app. The destination and the payment are similarly settled in advance through the hirer's smartphones. In the same way the location, timing, route and movement of the taxi can, amazingly, be seen on a dynamic screen map throughout. No cash is needed as the fare is paid electronically from the passenger's preregistered account.

In all these modes, drivers are normally – unless soon to be off duty – prepared to undertake longer journeys, for example to an airport or another town.
Some drivers like this as a long journey avoids an uncertain wait for the next fare.

Drivers of licensed hackney cabs are equipped to be paid by card as well as cash – and in London are now legally obliged to allow this; they provide a convenient small keyboard for passengers to input the necessary details, making it a quick and easy transaction. Minicab drivers expect cash, though recently some have started to accept cards, often with a stifled groan and sometimes an extra charge, after phoning their central office with the details, or pre-arranging it on their smartphones. This can be time-consuming so most people opt for cash.

Besides these common modes there are also special arrangements for long-term hiring by passengers or organisations. Businesses can set up regular accounts to avoid the fuss of cash payments and enable easier expenses tracking. Often this is for regular and predictable trips, for example 'the school runs' or driving commuters between home and railway station?

Such arrangements mean that drivers don't have to collect a fare on the day, fiddle with change, or write out a receipt, but instead get paid in due course by the business. On the other hand some drivers dislike this arrangement as they can't count on having cash in hand to pay for consumables on the day; so from the driver's viewpoint it cuts both ways.

The expected conventions of both passenger and driver behaviour vary according to the mode of hire. The hackney cab drivers are usually smartly dressed, even sometimes in uniform, and expect, though cannot demand, a tip. The passengers sit in the back – no other option – and the fare, with no room for negotiation, is calculated by the meter, visible to both driver and passenger as the drive proceeds. The payment can be either by cash or card and a receipt giving the date, amount, route and employing firm is normal practice.

Drivers in the licensed taxi ranks follow much the same procedure, again with meters and a rather higher fare than for minicabs. Passengers on the whole appreciate this, however, for the extra ease of finding a taxi when and where they want it, for example when arriving in an unfamiliar place by train, without the need for prior booking. For drivers there is the benefit that, though there may be a wait, they are pretty much guaranteed to get a fare rather than using up petrol in randomly and perhaps unproductively cruising the streets. The whole operation is more informal and relaxed with minicab. Though usually (not quite always) neatly if casually dressed, they are seldom in uniform. Passengers sit where they like, the doors are nit licked in transit, and fir alert passengers there can be some room for negotiation over the fare.

These then are the main conditions and constraints within which drivers expect to work – varied, but well known to them when they opt for a particular form of licence.

In Milton Keynes, a city: and the specific settings in which they work?

The main focus here is, as I have said, on the taxi drivers of the English city of Milton Keynes (MK), with the occasional comparative look elsewhere. But it is also worth repeating that the general patterns of taxi operation and driver conventions seem to be remarkably similar in urban settings throughout the world.

I chose Milton Keynes as it is where I live and study, where I see people getting taxis, and where for over ten years now I have regularly used them myself. It therefore, as I explained earlier, seemed natural to take the *Milton Keynes* taxi drivers as my focus, while touching on some experiences elsewhere to add some perspective. Let me follow this up then with some background about this particular urban setting.

Milton Keynes, still often referred to as a 'new city' though now in fact over 50 years old, had by the 2020s a population approaching a quarter of a million. It is a city I know well both from previous research studies (this will be my third book about Milton Keynes) and from having lived here since 1969: bringing up a family, living through the various life stages, and in recent years a frequent user of taxis. Milton Keynes is named after the ancient village of Milton, still there at the heart of the city, and the long-rooted local family of Keynes. It was founded in 1967 as part of the government's 'new towns' policy, designed principally to cater for the London overspill and situate them in pleasant surroundings. And they *were* – and are still – very pleasant.

The centuries-old 'Three Trees', a most ancient hostelry in the area. See Appendix 2 for an historic 'postcard' photo of this pub.

The Milton Keynes 'tree cathedral' modelled on Norwich Cathedral

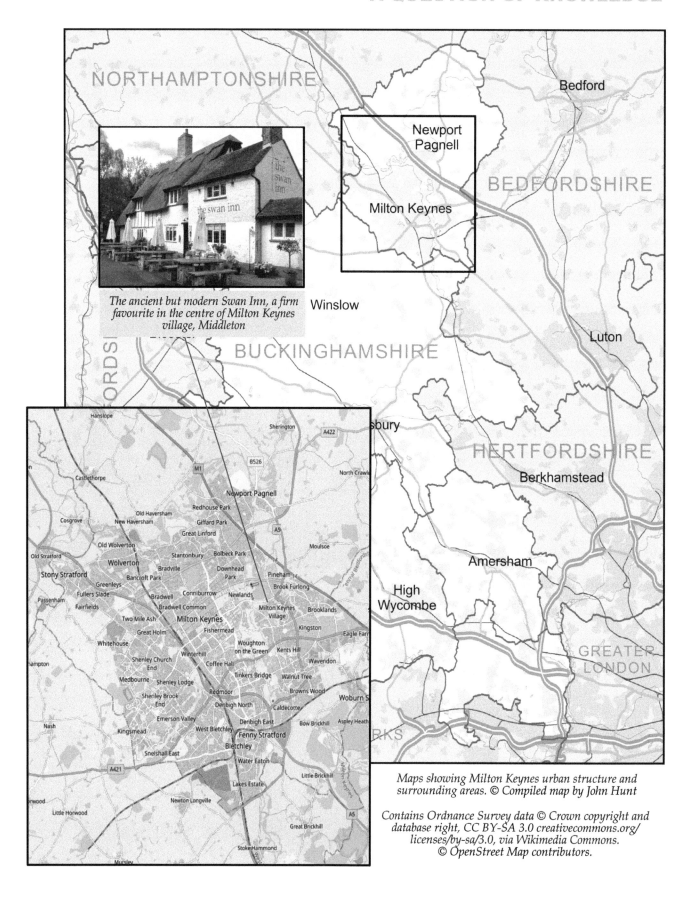

The ancient but modern Swan Inn, a firm favourite in the centre of Milton Keynes village, Middleton

Maps showing Milton Keynes urban structure and surrounding areas. © Compiled map by John Hunt

Contains Ordnance Survey data © Crown copyright and database right, CC BY-SA 3.0 creativecommons.org/licenses/by-sa/3.0, via Wikimedia Commons. © OpenStreet Map contributors.

So Milton Keynes emerged as a *green* city, with countryside and nature not just *around* but *within* the town. The city planners, somewhat unusually for the time, looked with great care not only at physical and economic development but at social and community development as well[12] –schools, playgrounds, social and religious centres and so on, all of which taxi drivers must know.

Floodplain Nature Reserve, North Milton Keynes

An early decision was that there should be a high degree of accessibility between all the activities which constitute a city– health, education, industry, recreation etc. Milton Keynes was to be multi-centred, with land use dispersed evenly throughout the city, but with a strong focus on *Central* Milton Keynes for certain citywide and sub-regional facilities, and for commercial office development, thus avoiding (up to a point) the peak-time pressure points that are common in older, 'radial', cities.

To this end, and very relevant for taxi drivers, a grid system of roads was developed that aimed to combine good general accessibility with flexibility to allow for growth and change. It was planned as a city of grid squares, with all intersections at ground level, approximately one kilometre apart. The plan stipulated the need for free and safe movement for pedestrians and cyclists, and, on the public transport side, that buses should run at frequent intervals with stops within easy walking distance for all local people. Another aim was to cherish both the ambience and the ancient buildings of local villages within the designated city area. This has indeed been fulfilled and become a notable feature of the city. Good transport connections were from the start to be of primary importance. The city was to be – and is – within easy reach of good road connections (the M1) and major rail networks (north-south and eventually east-west) .

Ancient and modern, Milton Keynes village now named Middleton. The building on the left was originally a bungolow, then rebuilt as a 'modern' house but with a thatch roof.

The city's layout – again very relevant for taxi drivers – is basically a grid pattern connecting squares of housing with local services such as first schools and religious, recreational and social centres (see Map on previous page). Convenient and humanly based as this undoubtedly is, it at the same time has given rise to some transport issues for residents due to the distances between local dwelling areas, the more so given the generous tree cover, river walks and parklands that separate them.

For the initially mainly young population walking and cycling are convenient and inexpensive options, and the city's unrivalled network of paths was specially created for this purpose.

---

[12] Further comment in Majevadia 2016

and responsive too, and with generally dependable arrival times, taxis have come into their own. Given the layout of Milton Keynes with its tree and park separated inhabited areas those without their own cars rely primarily on buses (not always convenient), and taxis; indeed even those who own cars sometimes prefer buses or taxis because of the cost and difficulty of parking in some areas, particularly in the crowded and expensive city centre.

Within the city, the first idea was of a light railway along the streets but that was abandoned for cost reasons. The early years saw a personalised 'Dial a bus' service, soon replaced by a more formal bus system – at first unpopular and with limited routes but recently with an excellent and frequent network, with routes convenient for most (but not all) residents and visitors. A recent move is to supplement the Electric Bus Project (having undergone a prototype electrified period) by transport that can be ordered on a personal basis from no more than 50 yards from where you are to your destination, free to disabled or over 60s passengers holding free bus passes.

As a result many taxi companies[13] have been established in the city, with some hundreds of licensed drivers – *too* many some drivers say – and taxis are plentifully available for hire.

But taxis are still in demand. Unlike other systems they take passengers in comfort and privacy both from and to the exact spot they wish. More rapid

Centre MK: Milton Keynes shopping centre

---

[13] Further details in Chapter 5

ON THE WAY

Chapter 4: Who are they?

The movement of people across countries is nowadays a worldwide occurrence, with the corollary that incomers need to find a way to support themselves as they dig in and lay the foundations for their children's future. For those with enough financial and/or human resources to somehow get control of a car –whether rented, bought outright, shared, afforded through a loan, or, for several, using a redundancy payment – taxi driving is the obvious course, and, it seems, there are always openings.

So it is scarcely surprising that a pre-ponderance of taxi drivers are immigrants from outside the country or, at the least, from outside the local area, making their way through the taxi industry. With a few exceptions, indeed, taxi drivers tend everywhere to be immigrants to the area whether from the same country or further afield. In many places, as in Milton Keynes, they come predominantly from the new Commonwealth with a few from Eastern Europe; in Cambridge and other older cities, they more often come from Eastern Europe.

I come from Bangladesh ...

'Not all those who wander are lost' (a taxi driver).

In Milton Keynes, then, taxi drivers or their families originated mainly from the Indian subcontinent and from Africa, with some from the Middle East, Eastern Europe and SriLanka, opting – or forced – to leave by difficult economic, political or military pressures to seek a better life abroad. On Milton Keynes streets there are drivers from the Congo, Nigeria, Ghana, many from India, Pakistan, Bangladesh and Kashmir, a few from Sri Lanka, driven here by the civil war, and from Iraq, Afghanistan and Iran

(including one who claimed to trace his ancestry back to the Persian royal family 5 centuries ago – and looked it too). There were a few from other countries, but not, as far as I could tell, from China, South America, the Caribbean, or Australasia.

Many had followed a spouse or family member here and a number had been born in this country and were now settled in Milton Keynes or the nearby Luton, a town particularly favoured by those from Pakistan and Bangladesh. As well as their current self-identification as fully British, almost all had taken British citizenship at the first allowed opportunity, and were usually fluent in English or well on the way to it. But they were also intensely loyal to their origin country. They sent money regularly, or at least whenever they could, and tried to save enough – a priority – to visit. They almost all had a spouse from the same background – often paving the way and a reason for their arrival – and whatever other languages they spoke (often very many),greatly valued their 'own' language and traditions.

Or again, a real if less tangible link to home, they were in contact with their deceased parents, a mother above all: 'Of course'. If you love someone you dream of them – who do you love more than a mother, the caring guarding knowing one?

Your father is not the same, he's more a friend, he knows everythingabout my life, but not for dreams'). The contact 'through dreams' was an experience I was many times seriously – and in a way convincingly – assured of. Some men did indeed say that they were still in a way aware of their deceased mother ('she tells me what I should do – of course, she is my mother') but did not speak of dreaming themselves; that was something for women ('I think my wife does and my sister). Even so they did not quarrel with the idea that dreams, for those who had them, were a touch of reality, and, at times, of 'home'.
All who could visited their original country and their family there, or planned to do so soon, yearly if possible. If a mother was living, that, predictably, was a special incentive, a real occasion for longing to visit, ideally to show off their children and take them to 'meet their cousins'.

Most drivers thus went 'back' every year or so. Most though not all said when asked that their children 'of course' knew their native language – 'their own' – and, it seemed to go without saying, the songs and dancing from home that went with it: 'Farsi (or Urdu or Akan or whatever …) is a beautiful language'.

Their backgrounds and experiences had often been hard – no 'smooth road' for them. But, typical immigrants, they held their hearts high and applied themselves and just got on with it. They were confident that through their own hard work now, the next generation would in the future be able to be establish themselves higher in the social scale.

So they were unquestioningly ambitious for their children. 'Will they be taxi drivers when they grow up?' I often asked. With only one exception among the many I questioned (he replied 'Maybe, we don't know yet'), the response was always either to throw up their

hands in horror, saying 'No' (the intonation conveying 'Of course not') or to laugh as if I had made the most ridiculous joke. Of all the responses I had in my hundreds of rides something like this was the most predictable.

When pressed they often went on, very seriously, 'We don't know yet, they're young, they will choose their own career'. It emerged pretty quickly that in practice the choices were already pretty much laid down for them: some highly qualified profession like medicine, law, dentistry, senior engineering, pharmacy, and the like. Nor were these pipe dreams: it was clear from those whose children were already grown up and in jobs, that these were indeed exactly the careers they were following (I saw no reason to doubt this, indeed had on occasion met some of these successful risers through the ranks).

A female aspirant!
(Warren 2003)

These were the wishes of fathers.
I assume that most mothers felt the same but had little chance to discuss this direct as I met very few female drivers. As far as I could tell there was overt discrimination against women drivers, provided of course they met the usual requirements. With drivers' flexible hours taxis might seem to offer a good career. In Milton Keynes at least and, I suspect, more widely too, only a few seemed to choose to do so – in the firm I know best, with hundreds of drivers, there were only two women. So even though, based no doubt due to women's greater confidence from their successful work during the war, and certainly now increasing in numbers, women are still relatively few in the taxi industry. Indeed they are treated as something to joke about, somehow strange and unexpected.

In one (female) driver's comment, 'I still get remarks like 'How nice to meet a woman driver for once, is it your husband's cab?' Huh'.

Given the countries of origin a large number were Muslims and by 2022 there were at least eight mosques across the city. There were also Hindus, a few Jehovah's Witnesses carrying on their typical doorstep missionising, and (mainly from Africa) a sizeable number of Christians, attending one or other of the many Pentecostal churches in the city. All knew of the city centre Christian ecumenical church, one of the known landmark taxi destinations/pickup places, though they were not always clear just what it stood for (open-minded they were mostly interested to hear); few if any had ever been into it.

For almost all of them, religion, whether or not conventionally observed, was a major factor in their lives, however diverse their backgrounds and personalities might otherwise be.

There were so many. There was Luke[14], now a dedicated church leader; the many part-time preachers; and the elderly grey-haired Pakistani who harangued me solidly for 30 minutes about the need to lead a good life – it was quite hard to extricate myself at the end. Another was 'Isaia', driving a smart black car, born in Sri Lanka driven out by the civil war; 'my mother is still there but I left when my brother was murdered by the army. Now here, driving – well, it's a job – and a good member of my [Pentecostal] church here '.

Those of Indian. Pakistani or Bangladeshi backgrounds mostly had parents who were farmers. They had generally helped on the farm as children (they'd loved it, in retrospect at least) and slipped easily into it again during their visits. A number still had, or would purchase or inherit, their own holding back there, and planned to return and farm or carry on a family business, in their homeland when they retired.

Others had worked with a parent's business abroad, sometimes inheriting it and/or

starting up something similar in the UK alongside their taxi work. Some, better off, continued to hold, or had built up, substantial possessions abroad. It so they might spend only part of the year as taxi drivers in the UK, maybe far exceeding the personal wealth of any of their passengers.

Rishi, typical of the East African Asian immigrants who from the 1960s have contributed so much to the British economy, counted both Kenya and India as his 'home country'. He kept up links with each, and worked alternately in Britain and with family members back in India.

This kind of dual identity was something quite often to be found among the MK taxi drivers.

How did I get here?

As a taxi driver told me 'A smooth road never made a good driver'. Like others from far-off countries, arriving after a difficult journey, he knew what he was talking about, and not just about driving – the 'no smooth road' was more than just a far-off metaphor'.

Delving into how and why they left their home country to come to Britain and in due course to Milton Keynes revealed remarkable stories of endurance and of perseverance against the odds – colourful and dramatic, often inspiring.

Scarcely surprisingly when you come to think of it they tended to tell these stories of travel and arrival in a deeply felt and dramatic way – almost as if they were novels but at the same time I had the clear impression they were in fact true memories, not now for the first time being told. They included episodes of strikes of bad but more often good luck, and in particular of helpful friends, contacts and amazing coincidences. A recurrent theme was of remarkably large sums of money having been borrowed – a debt of honour which must be repaid, even though, in a new, far-away,

---

[14] Here and elsewhere I have not used their real names (more on this in Appendix 1).

country, they could scarcely be hounded for it. Now safely established here, they also generally seemed to feel they were now honour bound to help others..

Of course there were no stories to be heard of the distress and ill fortune of those who for one reason or another, alas, had failed to get here. So we must just settle for the tales of those who succeeded.

Trials, traumas and triumphs

There were multiple stories of adventures and ingenuity and, in the end, as it were, glory, recalled with verve and excitement.

One MK driver the tale of how his migrant son had disappeared into the void, but then – coincidence, miracle – was found again from another migrant. The father was able track him down, and was filled with gratitude.

Another – let us call him Amir – had with a friend walked (yes, walked) all the way from Kurdistan in Iraq to England. It took two years. They had no money but somehow managed – they had to. They knocked on the doors of houses they came to and in most cases were given some food and a place to sleep to set them on the next leg of their – impossible you would think – journey.

His friend opted to stay in Europe but somehow (I don't know how) Amir, still penniless, managed to get across the English channel. He then found his way, again walking (imagine, all these London streets …) to central London. There he knocked on a door, this time of a small café. He asked if in return for working there all day he could sleep on the floor and have one meal. They agreed – bless them he said. After two days they offered him a paid job. At the end of a year he was the manager.

He then decided that the flexibility of taxi driving would suit him better and leave him free-er to do his own thing and get married.

Mastering the London taxi knowledge would take three to four years so he moved to Milton Keynes where it was quicker to get a license.

And now here he was, a quite well-off taxi driver, father of a family and a British citizen.

While proud to have made it in a new setting, he was modest in talking about his adventures and accomplishments. He was pleased of course now to be established in his new home, but it was clear that he would never forget Kurdistan or the sweet language and culture in which he grew up.

From Kurdistan again – an area whose people were then under dire threat from Saddam Hussein – came another nail-biting and dramatic story of repeated frustration and panic before final success.

With a friend he set off over the precipitous mountains, the only route for those like him to escape out of Kurdistan. They were stopped by guards and manhandled, their money taken. 'They we're hauling us off to throw us in prison, never to get out, but somehow God led me to say something to one of the guards in my language – it was his too, not many speak it. He let me go. Aah!'.

Then it was a long disheartened trudge back over the mountains, and months, years, raising more money. He sold all his remaining belongings – fairly substantial I gathered – to raise the thousands he knew would be needed.

'The only thing', he continued 'was to avoid the guards by flying out. The first hop was fairly easy. But then for a long haul flight to Britain – flying is safer than bus or boat or people smugglers when you'd get caught and turned back. But for that I somehow had to get a passport. So – more costs, huge. Then, look, a passport! I had it! It was in a Hungarian name of all things. I didn't know a word of the language but it was the only one I could get from the, er, passport suppliers.

I went with it to the international airport and – what a chance – one of my friends there knew the captain of one of the planes and he eased my way.

But first I had to go through the check-in, I had to show my passport, I was shaking inside, I was trembling all through my body – what if they questioned me in Hungarian! But – Ah, all was well, I was on the plane!'

By now established as a taxi driver in Milton Keynes he was working all hours to pay back his borrowed money.

I commented, to see what he would say, 'Surely they won't pursue you here in England?'

'Of course I will return it' he replied, and sped off smiling, eager for his next fare and a few more pounds towards his debt.

Another was Ahmed, a driver who greeted me with a gleaming smile when he picked me up. He had come to England from Afghanistan as an asylum seeker in 2002. Now, like many immigrant taxi drivers a British citizen, he ('yes, yes yes, I do!') loves it here.

But as he explained it was not easy getting here or finding a job and settling in. He had with a struggle managed to raise the money for the journey with the help of friends ('you have to borrow of course – and pay them back'). Then there was the notoriously formidable step of getting through the UK border post: 'That was a very very bad time. But in the end, in the end, in the end, the security person said – 'yes'!'

He managed to get a job in the Chocolate Factory in Birmingham – 'I love chocolate! and I was so lucky to know someone there, and then the company owner and the company checked me and with the help of a very good person I knew (thank you, thank you) they told me 'Yes everything is okay' '.

He still had to pay the agency who had arranged the initial contact but now he truly had a job and – essential and, not readily accorded to all asylum seekers, permission to work.

But more was needed. 'I liked the Chocolate Factory but I was too smart to stay there for long'. He had learned to drive before he left Afghanistan and heard from friends that the taxi market was doing well. 'So here driving a taxi. I like it all right. I get some good passengers and some not so good, but it puts food on the family's table'. He smiled.

'So far so good today', he added, 'if I'm lucky I end up with 12, 13, 15 jobs and not too much waiting around'.

Now established, he successfully applied for his wife and children to join him, and – 'wonderful', he said – had found somewhere to live.

He broke off as his in-cab phone sounded: 'Good news, somebody else wants me: another job', and making sure I'd got out safely and was on the way down my drive, he sped off with another smile.

Others had it easier, specially if they had a brother or family other member already here. A surprising number had a military background on their parents' or grandparents' side ('he was in the British Army'). This gave them an interest in coming to 'the old country' and stronger standing for entry. They often had an easier time when they arrived too – an established network, often a place to live while they got properly settled, contacts for a job, and, important, financial help, either as a loan or outright, with buying or sharing a car so they could get straight into taxi driving once they'd got a licence and were signed up with a local taxi business. Settled – but still with regular visits to their homeland.

All these experiences, all these unique, created, lives …

Chapter 5: The job

Many but not all drivers said they liked the job of taxi driving. Sometimes this was just from the pleasure of driving and having control of a car. Sometimes it was their interaction with the passengers. Most often it was 'its flexibility'.

For others – 'Well, it's a job'. For them, driving was a necessity – not necessarily an unpleasant one – rather than a passion: 'I mean its not really – well it can be at times but then I suppose any job can – anyway its just a line of business you know, you just get to understand that and it puts food on the family table'.

Getting into it

Sometimes taxi driving was in the family. Among London drivers Philip Warren (2003) was not unique in his four-generation taxi-driving heritage. But in Milton Keynes, predominantly immigrants after all, most drivers had turned to taxi driving and chosen which taxi company to join up not as the result of family tradition or even a careful comparison of opportunities or companies ('they're much of a muchness') but – as so often happens in life – through a friend or relative who had done so. As well of course they needed to have access to a car – purchased, rented, shared or borrowed – a driving licence and some free time.

Many immigrants arrive in Britain with nothing and, typically, begin in street marketing or the bottom of the rag trade; some get no further, others build up a fortune. Others still, themselves immigrants or descended from immigrant families, try to carry on a trade in which they already have experience, such as working in the restaurant industry (very common) or jobs locally regarded as unskilled like building, supermarket, warehouse and delivery work. But if they are able to drive, speak reasonable English and have a personable demeanour, taxi driving – freelance and flexible – is often been the obvious choice. For many 'to be honest, I just kind of fell into it'.

Taxi driving furthermore is commonly a way to supplement other income without losing your options, to gain useful experience, and to earn some extra cash while not being tied down. Indeed in Britain and perhaps elsewhere it is one of the top free lance additional occupations, made possible by the increasing number of minicab taxis in demand. Indeed in England something like one in a hundred people may be driving a taxi to supplement their other income.

> **Most popular jobs**
> Shop assistant 1,079,000
> Care worker 759,000
> Nurse 639,000
> Cleaner 575,000
> Catering assistant 507,000
> Warehouse worker 488,000
> Book-keeping 434,000
> Primary teacher 425,000
> Secondary teacher 382,000
> Taxi driver 363,000
> ONS April-June 2018

Most popular additional jobs
Office of National Statistics, UK, 2018

Looked at from the other end it is, then, not surprising that many taxi drivers, including those in Milton Keynes, have, or have had, parallel or additional careers to driving in the past or present. Many for example are or have been not just drivers but also students, chefs, delivery men, pastors, musicians – or, again, a trainee minister, manager, heavy good vehicle driver, gymnast[15]. A leading politician in today's cabinet recounts how, when in his youth his immigrant father's business collapsed, he was prepared to drive a taxi to put food on the family table; a soldier in the Ukraine defending army had been a taxi driver; even Putin for some years, it is said, drove a taxi.

Despite some legal controversies over the status of Uber drivers, the drivers studied here (who, remember exclude workers formally

---

[15] Examples and further discussion in Chapter 9.

employed by businesses or wealthy individuals as chauffeurs or delivery people) are, and regard themselves as, freelance and self-employed. The downside of no holiday or sick pay, or redundancy payment is, for them, balanced by the flexibility of freelance working and the freedom to choose their own hours. I was consistently told that this was the main advantage of being a taxi driver other work. ' my own master'. They are independent, not tied into a permanent job or its conditions.

To become a taxi driver, as immigrant would-be drivers soon found, you must be in the relevant country with the right to work there, you must be able to drive, and to have passed a recognised driving test. You must somehow have access to a car, have good health and eyesight, no criminal record, and several other requirements. Then there was the special 'taxi driver assessment' with centres throughout the country[16]. These explained how to apply, the paperwork to bring, and the requirements of the special taxi driving test which included not just practical skills but knowledge of the Highway Code and an eyesight test, summarised in official guidance documents as:

- All taxi drivers need to be licensed and display their license clearly in their vehicle whenever they are working. The licensing conditions depend on the local council authority, but applicants are generally required to:
- Be at least 21 years of age.
- Hold a full UK driver's license.
- Undergo a CRB check.
- Demonstrate proof that they have the right to live and work in the UK.
- Pass an area knowledge test.
- Go through an in depth medical examination by a nominated GP.
- Complete a specialised taxi driving test, which includes a written exam, eye-sight test and practical assessment.
- Self-employed taxi drivers will need to either own their own vehicle, or hire a vehicle for a weekly or monthly cost. It is your responsibility as a taxi driver to make sure the vehicle fits the standards set by your local council, which are there to ensure that your vehicle is safe and fit for purpose. Contact your local authority for more information.
- Although there is no formal training required to become a taxi driver there are certain skills that will be required of you:
- Customer service skills – As a taxi driver you will meet some weird and wonderful people. It is important to know how to handle difficult, disruptive or intoxicated individuals to ensure that you and your passengers arrive at the destination safely. Tips are not to be sniffed at, as once you start working you will soon find out that the tips you receive for providing a friendly and professional service will soon add up into an impressive sum.
- A good sense of direction – One of the main reasons why people favour a taxi service over public transport is because of time pressures, so your passengers will expect you to take them to their desired destination by the quickest route possible. Make sure that you know the area you are working in like the back of your hand so any road closures or traffic incidents won't cause too much disruption. Remember, customers will not be impressed if you take them on the scenic route while the meter is running!
- Don't be short changed – Most people will pay their taxi fare in cash and so being able to count small change before your customer has jumped out will prevent an absent minded customer passing you a tenner instead of a twenty.
- Be fit and healthy – Taxi drivers are not just required to transport their passengers from A to B, but also their luggage. Part of providing a good service (and a good way of earning tips!) is being able to assist customers with loading and retrieving their luggage.

---

[16] mytaxitest.co.uk/test-centres/

On top of this was the test of the driver's knowledge of all the roads in the local area where he planned to work. This final test, always demanding, was notoriously hardest for drivers who wanted a London black cab licence either on its own or in addition to a local licence: – which of course they must always display as proof of their status.

Them

They may not be fully aware of them all, but many external forces impact on drivers' lives. First and most obvious is the government, in other words the legal regulations about what drivers can and cannot do and how they must behave. This is a serious business for drivers, necessarily taken to heart. Its observance by drivers is in part monitored by the police, agents of the law, who are among the important forces in the drivers' conduct of their working lives. Police have an eye to such aspects as drivers' visible display of their licence and their keeping to the rules of the road, speed limits and lighting up times, seat belts, no driving while drunk or in an old or unsound car, and a host of similar regulations. There are also somewhat more elusive guidelines, including those of the national Highway Code and less codified conventions to do with courtesy and

consideration for others which drivers would be foolish to ignore .

Whether legal or merely a matter of socially approved convention and road courtesy, drivers as I say take all this very seriously. They have to. Transgressing the rules would risk losing their licence, and thus their livelihood. Drivers tend to have a sense of humour about their circumstances and sometimes joke light heartedly about all this. Take this list of mock 'commandments', some related to legal requirements, some just sensible and practical rules of the road – but serious nevertheless:

The 10 Commandments of Road Safety

1. Thou shalt not gaze at thy phone.
You're not fooling anyone if you are staring at your crotch with a smile. Keep your eyes off your damn phone when you are driving! If you are using your phone while driving you deserve a massive punch in the throat.

2. Thou shalt not throweth trash out of the window.
Are you on your way to a 'binless' planet? A planet where there is no trash and trash cans? No, you are not on your way to magical 'trashless' Narnia; stop throwing your crap out of the car and just keep it till your next stop to dispose it properly.

3. Thou shalt not – nev'r – drive intoxicated.
Do not even begin to argue. Do not touch those car keys if you are over the limit, even if you are just slightly over the limited. Uber. Call a taxi. Get a lift with a friend. Dammit people, if you want to do adult things, then act like one.

4. Thou shalt not taketh any chances.
There is a blind curve in front of you, there is a hill, there is line prohibiting you from overtaking the car in front of you. But do you listen? No! Who do you think you are? Tarzan? Then go swing in a tree. Don't take chances.

[17] Spelled out in detail in gov.uk/government/publications/private-hire-and-hackney-carriage-licensing-open-letter-to-local-authorities/regulation-of-taxis-and-private-hire-vehicles-understanding-the-impact-on-competition

5. Thou shalt buckle up thy kids.
Parents, parents, parents. We all get it, kids want to sit on your lap but that's recklessly stupid and if you allow it then you are recklessly stupid. Yes you. Buckle and secure your kid in his or her seat. Hand out lollipops or whatever to keep them happy, but your lap is not a place for a kid in a moving car.

6. Thou shalt not drive on thy brights.
Stop blinding other drivers with your brights. Also, creators of all these fancy new cars, are all of you engineers challenged in the eye region? What's up with the new white-blue lights? It's even worse than an old car on brights. No man, go back to the drawing board and dim it!

7. Thou shalt not drive with one light or with faulty lights.
What are you? A motorbike? A fast bicycle? A firefly with a really big bum? Who knows when only light is working. Make sure both lights are in order when you get on the road. Please. Thank you. Goodbye.

8. Thou shalt adhere to the speed limit.
Speed limits are actually there for a reason. Heaven knows why people think it doesn't apply to them. Also, people with fancy cars, just keep in mind that even though your speed-o-meter goes up to 260 km/h, the speed limit applies to you as well. Stop showing off. No one is impressed.

9. Thou shalt keepeth thy distance.
If I can read your license plate number in my rear view mirror then you are too close. If you are driving 80km/h and 8 cars can't fit in the distance between me and you, please tell me, what will happen if I have to stop suddenly? Will your car's bonnet meet my car's boot? STOP driving on my arse. I will fart in your face.

10. Thou shalt practice patience.
Trucks are the best way to practice your patience; if they can't go faster, they can't help

it. Be patient if you can't pass a truck and wait until you know it is safe. Patience can be a life-saver'.

The local council has a direct and known impact on drivers which, it is obvious when you look at their detailed requirements, they exercise with great care. It is they who run the tests necessary to obtain a licence, regulate the number of taxis allowed in the area, maintain the roads (the awkward temporary road closures too) and issue local regulations. It is to them that drivers licensed to join the taxi ranks owe their licences and to them – not, as with the minicab drivers, to the local taxi companies – that such drivers must pay a fee.

Involvement with the police or local council can be complex, with potentially large impacts on a driver's livelihood. Here is how a Milton Keynes female taxi driver, dependent on her taxi work to feed herself and her family, described her experience some years ago.

'I knew that I had reached a fairly dangerous point for me when my car reached an age when it couldn't be re-plated [licensed] by the council. Because you are only allowed to use cars as taxis up to an age, and I didn't have the where with all for a new one. And the thought went through my head, 'Oh, I know what I will do, I will go to so and so, because he will be able to get me a nicked car'. And the moment I thought that thought, I thought 'Hang on, what are you saying?'

'And that is actually when I made the decision to leave. Because even though I didn't do the things that they did, by association I felt uncomfortable with it. And while purely as individuals many of these people were charming, they would come into my home, they would be talking, and my children would be here absorbing thoughts, it is hard to say. I mean kids aren't stupid, kids know what is going on, and I thought 'No, how can I on the one hand say to my children 'It is wrong to steal, it is wrong to take drugs, it is wrong to threaten someone with a shot gun just because they haven't paid you your fare', and then say but it is OK for these people to come into my home and talk about it' – because it isn't really OK is it? I had got into it slowly, you don't realise because it is so pervasive'.

A very visible player in the game is thus the local council. It is they who control both the number of taxis allowed in the area and the test taxi drivers have to pass to get a license and thus be allowed to drive a taxi at all.

How about wider alliances? In Britain the interests of many professions are represented by a union or unions. This did not actually seem to be much of a factor for drivers however, in Milton Keynes at least. There are taxi drivers associations like the London based Licensed Taxi Drivers Association Ltd and the National Taxi Association which no doubt have been involved in negotiating for better driver conditions, but local drivers seemed little aware of them. When I asked I got (hesitant) answers like – 'I think there is, I'm not sure', 'They don't do anything for us do they', 'I don't know what they do, do I …'. In Milton Keynes at any rate, with the possible exception of Uber drivers, these unions seemed to have little if any felt impact on drivers' lives.

Another factor is the local transport policy and road layout which clearly affects the setting in which drivers operate. In Milton Keynes, housing settlements are far apart, with attractive but divisive fields and parks between. Households without a car or other personal transport (indeed without a second car when one partner is away at work with the first) are isolated and depend on either a bus – not always conveniently routed – or a taxi for shopping, work or social contact. It's a taxi-friendly city therefore as evinced by the literally hundreds of taxis on its streets. Drivers are affected too by things going on at the national level, if only indirectly. The relative newcomer Uber is a big player here.

There are particular – and highly controversial – limitations on where they are allowed to operate. Being new, Uber is often seen as bringing in 'unfair' new competition to traditional taxi drivers through having (arguably) laxer driver regulation and acceptance. They aggressively tout for new drivers, something that, especially in years following the lockdown due to the covid epidemic years, are felt to be somewhat short supply. They send out clever adverts in such terms as, in an online blog, 'Uber wouldn't be Uber without the drivers that use our platform. They're at the heart of everything we do as a business. That's why we've been working hard to ensure they have the support and protections they need and the flexibility they want...

What's new in 2021

From 16th March this year, we made a commitment that drivers using Uber would immediately be entitled to a number of worker protections whilst driving on the Uber App:

- National Living Wage: Every driver is guaranteed to earn at least the National Living Wage, although they can and do earn more. This is an earnings floor, not a ceiling, and most drivers regularly exceed the National Living Wage in the pay they take home.
- Holiday Pay: Drivers now receive holidaypay.They get paid an additional 12.07% of their earnings, paid each week, making it easier to plan some much needed downtime with family and friends.
- Pension Contributions: A pension plan will be available for all eligible drivers, which we'll be sharing more details about in the coming months. It'll include contributions from Uber and drivers, helping drivers plan ahead and build a nest egg for the future.

---

[18] partners.24.com/safety24/the-10-commandments-of-road-safety/index.html/

One of these people has access to free Open University courses through work

The other one is in the back seat

Flexibility with benefits   Uber

'We have also joined forces with GMB Union in a groundbreaking trade union recognition deal. This means that drivers will retain the freedom to choose if, when and where they drive whilst also having the choice to be represented by GMB.

All this, only on Uber

They have some success, it seems, as by 2022 Uber is believed to have around 70,000 drivers in the United Kingdom. At the international level too, little though local drivers may be aware of it, Uber has been involved in long political, some say shady, dealings which may have a long term potential to impact on the taxi industry more generally even if little felt locally, for the moment at least.

That brings us to the local taxi companies, important and visible forces in drivers' everyday lives. That is what we must get to next.

The local taxi companies

Apart from the hackney licensed 'black cabs' who can pick up their passengers on the street (pretty much limited to London) and at recognised taxi ranks, drivers, minicab drivers, the majority in most towns, certainly Milton Keynes, find their passengers by signing up with a local taxi company. Mostly this is one based in or near their general locality, though there are also the international companies of Uber or Bolt. Without being signed up with one or more taxi firms drivers cannot in effect get an income. Apart from the passengers, these local taxi companies are thus the most important factor in a minicab driver's life. They in their turn are dependent on their drivers, and keen to recruit both drivers and other related employees.

Recruitment

Here, for example, is a recruitment advert from Royal Cabs, one of the leading MK taxi firms:

Royal Cars are committed to serving the community of Oxfordshire in a professional and timely manner. We are constantly looking to expand our team are interested in owner drivers with modern and well maintained vehicles, a 1st class customer service and a hard working ethic. All Royal Cars drivers must have a valid Private Hire or Hackney Carriage badge issued by one of the local Districts in Oxfordshire (Oxford City Council, Vale of White Horse District Council, Cherwell District Council, South Oxfordshire District Council and West Oxfordshire District Council). If you have a valid Private Hire or Hackney Carriage badge but do not have your own vehicle, please get in touch with our Fleet Manager, as we do have vehicles available for hire.

Telephonists

Part time telephonist positions are available throughout the year. Telephonists are an integral part of our business and the first point of contact for the majority of our customers. The main duty of a telephonist is to receive calls in a professional and courteous manner, making booking onto the central dispatch system and deal with any queries as best as possible. Telephonist must be well mannered, motivated and have the ability to work well within the team.

There is more than one arrangement between driver and company. Some taxi drivers drive their own car. In that case they themselves were responsible for its maintenance, insurance, petrol, road tax and any further expenses, and paid a weekly amount to the operating firm for managing the bookings, either as a separate fee or – now increasingly the case – an automatically deducted percentage of their earnings of around 15-20% taken off the payment for each trip.

---

[19] uber.com/en-GB/blog/only-on-uber/

44

A similar arrangement applied to working direct with Uber and Bolt with the difference that with them the only option was to own your vehicle and booking details and payments were operated online rather than through the driver's smartphone connection to a local company.

It was generally accepted that if you could find the purchase money, quite often with support from your family, it was good to have your car. It was an investment that could if necessary be sold or part-exchanged for another. Your own car lowered the amount paid to the taxi company and made it simpler to change firms or even to leave the taxi industry altogether but still own a car.

The other arrangement is to lease your car from the taxi company. This too had advantages for drivers. The company looked after expenses such as road tax, insurance and maintenance, for which the driver paid the company a weekly fee (rising over the years), or up to 40% or so of their fare income. It meant that the driver could, without bother or separate payment, count on a well maintained and (usually) expensive car of high quality. Nowadays the car is increasingly likely to be hybrid or electric thus keeping the fuel costs down. Relatively few could afford to buy such expensive cars outright so leasing proved to be a popular and good-value arrangement for drivers.

A further twist on this is for a driver to lease a car elsewhere, at a cheaper rate than from one of the taxi companies. This enabled him to sign up for the 'owning his own car' deal without the cost of an outright purchase.

When a driver is ready to take fares that day he signs in on his smart phone with the company operator or, where applicable, Internet link to say that he is available. He may have to wait around for a fare as the operator contacts the vehicle nearest to the pick-up spot with the passengers's name and

destination, automatically contacting the passenger to confirm the booking details and, in due course, report that the taxi had been dispatched and, then arrived.

If the driver wants to take a break, as for a meal or special occasion or to collect children from school etc he lets the dispatcher know not to get him any bookings for the moment. He then reports back when he is available. 'No problem about doing that ', I was told 'I'm my own master – though you're not very popular if you keep doing it and messing them up all through the day'.

Besides these common modes there were also special arrangements for long-term hiring by passengers or organisations.

Businesses sometimes set up regular accounts to avoid the fuss of cash payments and enable easier expenses tracking. This meant that passengers did not have to pay on the day. This was a popular arrangement for commuters who wished to have a taxi always

[20] bbc.co.uk/news/business-62057321/

[21] allthingsbusiness.co.uk/2021/03/31/bolt-launches-ride-hailing-service-in-milton-keynes/ royal-cars.com/oxford-taxi-company-jobs/

available for them at a particular time – often rush hour –without the fuss of ordering each time from scratch. It was also good for regular trips like daily school runs and hospital, prison, expedition, or prison transport, predictable trips that it was convenient to arrange centrally, sometimes with the same, regular, driver.

The taxi companies, key to how drivers operated in Milton Keynes, changed over time. By 2022, besides some smaller firms and a few specialising in 'Executive chauffeur-driven luxury' and such, there were at the time of my research around half a dozen leading companies[22] plus a few smaller or ephemeral ones.

Earlier ones had been taken over or faded out. Each offered 'fast, comfortable and reliable service' or words to that effect. They often also served, or in some cases were based In, nearby towns like Oxford or Northampton, and operated hundreds of vehicles. There were also some firms, working on much the same general lines, specialising in airport or other longer trips, bookable in the same way.

ROYAL 001 CABS

AIRPORT PRICES	Saloon	6 Seater	8 Seater
LUTON	£30	£40	£50
HEATHROW T1,2,3	£60	£70	£80
HEATHROW T4,5	£65	£75	£85
BIRMINGHAM	£65	£75	£85
EAST MIDLANDS	£70	£80	£90
STANSTED	£70	£80	£90
GATWICK	£90	£100	£11

PRICES FROM MILTON KEYNES
(PRICES EXCLUDE AIRPORT CHARGES)

01908 563 563
WWW.001ROYALCABS.CO.U

For local companies drivers are connected by a smartphone phone in their cabs to their operator/dispatcher from whom they receive bookings (for Uber and Bolt it is through an internet App).

The taxi nearest to the pick-up address is dispatched and a text message sent to the passenger confirming the booking and, in due course the taxi's dispatch and arrival (Bolt and Uber passengers can instead track it on the their phone display, as in the image here – automatic, no need for the driver to enter it).

According to one driver, some of the telephone dispatchers are suspected of having 'favourites' to whom they unfairly give jobs ahead of other drivers and whom it is therefore worth wooing by gifts of scent or chocolates. This is the kind of thing that, humans being what they are, could well happen so surmises are not surprising, but when asked about it just about all drivers vehemently (and I would think rightly) denied this and took the dispatchers' fairness for granted. This of course mattered in a situation where there was competition between drivers for fares and some might end up at the close of the day with few or even no jobs.

Many drivers complained about what they described as increasing local competition. They said too many firms and too many drivers were allowed in Milton Keynes, the situation, they claimed, getting worse every year; they now had to work longer hours to make ends meet. In fact, with the covid lockdown, the numbers have actually declined in recent years. However, whatever the truth of that, minicab drivers certainly looked unsympathetically at Uber and station rank drivers: 'They are our competitors'. True enough.

Apart from the prepaid trips, at the end of the journey the driver must tell the passenger the due amount and this is (except from the occasional 'bilker' described later[23]) paid to the driver, with or (more normal for minicab drivers) without a tip. Most companies deduct a percentage but otherwise the fare is for the driver to keep.

The taxi companies themselves are reputed to do very well. During my research, one long-established Bletchley taxi company was sold

---

[22] In 2022 these included among others the closely connected Skyline and Starline; 001Royal Cabs; Milton Keynes Taxis; Speedline; 247 Taxiline Milton Keynes. At the start of my research the Bletchley-based Raffles had for many years been the leading and long established firm, but it was then bought out by a more distant based firm, which was in turn taken over by Skyline.

[23] Bilkers: explained in Chapter 6.

to another taxi firm for, I was told, £200,000, and another for £1 million. This to me was at first thought incredible – how could running a down to earth local taxi service be worth anything like that?

But it was pointed out to me that, in addition to each company owning a large fleet of the cars – a good investment in itself – it received a good weekly fee of £150-250 from each driver with a leased car every week whether or not it was being driven that week – quickly mounting up when you reckon that they had 50 and 200 drivers working for them respectively at the time of the sale. And then as well there were the fees from the drivers who owned their own cars.

Against this the companies had relatively small expenses. There was the cost for the 24-hour dispatch operation, maintenance for the leased out cars by their own mechanics and workshop, and other running expenses for the cars they owned and rented out.

They had none of course for those owned by drivers (the drivers were responsible for fuel costs and for the expenses associated with the requirements of qualifying as taxi drivers).

In addition the sellers were transferring the solid 'good will' of their established position in the local taxi industry, a working dispatch system with knowledgeable dispatchers, a roster of trained and experienced drivers, and hundreds of faithful customers.

Considering all that, the purchase price was not after all so surprising. Even the weekly income would have been substantial, let alone the value of the cars and the yearly profit. One driver surmised – rightly or wrongly – that all the local companies were owned by wealthy Pakistanis with the biggest firm probably pulling in £1 million a week: as he concluded with a wry smile, 'When the big fish are swimming around, those big fish there, the little fish don't know'.

I had at first been astounded when told that running taxis was a 'highly lucrative business'. no longer surprised.

The purchaser of the long-established Bletchley firm, Raffles, was for a time regarded as the 'up and coming company'. But they were quite soon themselves taken over, perhaps to even greater profit. The same was doubtless so with the repeated turnovers that I observed over the years.Amidst this changing jungle the drivers continued their usual work, taking on and delivering passengers according to their accustomed conventions.

Earnings

Taxi drivers' incomes came from the fares paid by their passengers. The due amounts varied over time and to an extent between companies, but, as an example, in Milton Keynes most journeys within the city (the most common form) lasted 20-30 minutes for which minicab drivers were paid £6-9 (a bit more for hackney cab drivers). There was a minimum charge, however short the journey, of £2.50-£3 and a waiting time of around 30p per minute. It cost more at night or during public holidays. Longer journeys, like to Heathrow or other airports, took upwards of an hour for which, depending on the distance, the driver could count on around £60-£100.

If the car was leased from the company the fee or percentage due from the driver was higher but insurance, maintenance, depreciation, road tax and other expenses were paid by the company; those who owned their own cars (for which of course they had had to produce or borrow the quite hefty purchase price) covered such expenses themselves.

All in all, apart from the occasional but always possible evasion by non-payers, the drivers could count on a fair monetary reward for their work. Charges were set either by meter or by a printed or electronic list which, if necessary, the driver could consult. They were then paid, pretty much without argument, by cash or card or electronically.

Fares mostly tended to be the same across the different firms, indeed to a degree coordinated. In December 2016 for example one firm sent round a text message to their passengers saying their fares were remaining at 'our usual low level' over Christmas – but all firms were actually charging the same. Another year all the local companies simultaneously put up fares by £1 over the break, to reduce them again simultaneously a few weeks later.

But given that at any one time there were, in Milton Keynes, many hundreds of drivers looking for fares, there was always competition for passengers. At various times different companies were claiming on their web pages, not always accurately, to be 'the cheapest'. At a more elusive level, certain enterprising drivers charged more than the standard fare, something it was hard for even a knowing passenger, faced with this at the end of a trip, to resist.

A driver's regular take-home pay varied not so much on the arrangement with their operating company – things balanced out pretty much whichever the detailed method – but rather on how many hours they worked a week. Some worked pretty much full time, though still able to choose take off time for special events, family commitments or occasions such as the great Islamic festivals (during Ramadan or even just on Fridays drivers were often thin on the ground). Also many drivers had regular or sporadic additional jobs and sometimes spent many weeks on other things, including vacations, illness, accidents – being freelancers they received no pay for such, whatever the reason – or visits to their home countries. Sometimes indeed taxi driving was, for them, just an optional and occasional sideline.

With all these variations, together with the rising cost of living over the last years, stating some definitive 'average' amount for drivers' earnings risks being misleading. Furthermore money is always a sensitive subject and one on which drivers, though not refusing to speak, did not readily expand. However I was pretty consistently told when I probed for the average amount of their weekly take-home pay after expenses that it was '£100'. Then, again, as if an afterthought 'more if I work more hours'. This sum remained the same all through a five year period when prices were continually rising.

This was so commonly the response that I came to the conclusion that '£100' was, so to speak, a symbolic rather than literal amount. It was defined in essence (as it was often further explained to me) as 'enough to put food on the table', this apparently being so whether the family was just the driver and spouse, or a number of hungry children with their own unavoidable expenses.

A good symbolic sum – and why not? But judging from what some were prepared to divulge, it was well short of the actual weekly amount. When pressed, some gave much higher figures, though again with the qualification 'it depends how many hours I work'. Many spoke of holidays abroad or visits to their home country every couple of years, sometimes accompanied by their children – scarcely a cheap regular commitment.

So, to get more realistic, in 2022, after the dearth of the previous two years' covid lockdown when many turned to alternative jobs, many drivers said that if they worked an average number of hours a weeks – around 35-40 – their take-home pay after expenses was around £400-500, 'more if I work longer'. An Uber driver getting £500 for a roughly 40 hour five-day week in 2022 said that if he worked longer hours he could easily raise this to £1000. The minicab drivers sometimes, as well as a local licence, had additionally gained the more expensive London minicab qualification, and split their time between, Milton Keynes and London. In this way they could greatly boost their income since in London the take-home amount tended to be higher.

This commonly mentioned figure of £400-500 for the weekly take-home pay fitted more or less with national calculations estimating a freelance taxi driver's average income as £25,000 per annum[24] – not that local taxi drivers ever seemed to think of it in per annum terms. 'Weekly' rather than yearly terms is what they lived by. After all 'If you're ill you don't get any holiday pay, you have to manage everything yourself as you go, and go on paying the company weekly fee too'.

All in all, drivers seem to feel that, with the potential problems inherent in any line of work, they get a fair whack of the whip in their chosen profession, and a reasonable recompense for the hours they work – especially if in the course of it they meet interesting and not too demanding passengers.

Chapter 6: Ignorant riff raff …

Taxi drivers feel that they are often looked down on as uneducated, possible cheats, and without money or prospects. That is, indeed, one popular view of taxi drivers, fuelled further by inbuilt, not necessarily fully conscious, xenophobic and racist attitudes against immigrants.

When asked directly it seems many people do not really think this. Even if they do, they still confidently rely on taxis, and avoid any personal curiosity about their driver that might allay those views. So getting at their real attitudes is complex, elusive. But whatever that case, this negative picture generally was – and is – far from the truth.

Ignorant?

Overall – *not* so. It is true that many had only basic education – 'just school … ', I was quite often told, thus leaving them, as they said,

with ' few options'. But taken as a whole taxi drivers' educational qualifications would seem, if anything, to be higher than those of the general population. Many of the MK drivers were graduates or, for all they now chose to earn a living by driving taxis, held advanced technical or craft qualifications from their original countries. Many already had MBAs or other postgraduate degrees and/or had had senior management experience. One had post-doctoral qualifications in nuclear physics but for now preferred the flexibility of a taxi-driver's life, while Rayan – appropriate name – had been a nationally admired fine jewellery craftsman in Pakistan. His qualifications were unrecognised in this country, so he was forbidden to practise here and was filling in time as a driver.

It is worth remembering too that educational institutions are not the only route to learning. Many drivers were painstakingly improving their English fluency by various means: reading, investigating through the web, learning as they went. I recall a driver from the Congo whose English, while just adequate for what was needed, was really quite poor – but when, by an unusual chance, I met him again some months later he was near-fluent, I'm not sure through what means. Some of those with relatively little formal education were taking advantage of local or national courses to improve their qualifications.

James, for example, regretted he had not stayed on at school after the minimum, or, like his friends, travelled the world. Instead, having for a time run his own company, he had turned to taxi driving where he liked picking the brains of interesting passengers and in this way adding to his learning. He cross-examined me closely about the meaning of 'anthropology' and in what ways it might be different from 'theology'. He drove off looking satisfied, something new learnt.

I had a similar close examination from another about the exact constitutional position of

---

[24] uk.indeed.com/career/taxi-driver/salaries

Northern Ireland and the precise meaning of its border, and, with a female driver from Bulgaria, a pleasant and well informed interchange about Indo-European languages and their subdivisions and interrelations.

Amari (a name meaning 'possesses great strength' from an Ivory Coast family, was brought up in Germany, so spoke German, French and a West African language. Educated at a German military academy, he had spent 21 years as a heavy goods vehicle driver in the German army. 'I'm now retired with a good pension, and enjoy occasional driving in the UK where it's good to have joined other members of my family here'. He was married to the daughter of the Ivory Coast Ambassador to Germany.

Another driver proudly showed me photos of his family in his phone: his wife (in a professional job), his son just finishing an MA this year, his eldest daughter a journalist, his second daughter specialising in languages: she can now, he told me, speak German, French, Spanish, English, and Chinese. I remember too the charming Ramon, called 'his gift to me' by his grandfather (also named Ramon). He had come to Britain on a work permit 26 years ago from India where he had been a senior Manager in engineering trading, then similarly in the UK. He said that he was the 'least educated of the family; my father and my sister are Directors of international companies, so is my wife'. He went on – *not* the 'ignorant unintellectual stereotype of taxi drivers – 'I read one and half hours every day, then more when I get home'.

Then there was Azir, resplendent in his crisp white robe ('a mark of respect' for Friday) who was writing stories and exploring the possibility of publishing them, and the initially taciturn Akbar who, once he saw I might be a kindred spirit, revealed an all-absorbing interest in history and cross-examined me exhaustively about Irish history. Another was deep into researching local

history, another specialising in Punjabi sources about the Mogul empire.

Kazun took a different line. He was passionate about the history of his native Sri Lanka which he had spent years researching, tracing it back to 25,000 years ago when, he claimed, a great Sumerian empire stretched the world from Ireland to New Zealand. He supported this historical theory from his detailed research into New Zealand place names, many of which, he held, originated in Sri Lankan Tamil. He was indeed impressive as his recounted his detailed research (well, there have been wilder theories before now, not least among the learned!).

Not exactly 'uneducated ignoramuses'.

Further, and this was no accident, *education* was for them the talisman, the key for the next generation to attain their way up. Time after time it emerged that for today's immigrant taxi drivers, education was, above all things, the highest value. The drivers' children were, and were encouraged to be, hard working and successful in school, almost invariably already in, or confidently expected to get, high-level professional jobs.

Their linguistic fluency was striking too, remarkable even for immigrants and no doubt honed in their interaction with their fellows of many origins, and with their variegated passengers. Many knew additional languages from having spent several years in other countries, most commonly Germany or Holland, on their way to Britain. All spoke and generally wrote their 'home' language(s) as well as English, and most knew many more – sometimes as many as five or six in addition.

In its recent application to be named an official 'City' Milton Keynes reported that 140 languages were spoken within its borders, including those of every Commonwealth nation.

It is likely that taxi drivers would figure prominently among these multilingual speakers. The driver Kamran for instance was fluent in five Asian languages plus Dutch and English, and said he could understand something of two more.

Many are expert too in the history and literature of their original country and an at first sight surprising number had published accounts of various kinds – informative, moving, human, witty – about their first hand experiences.

I was surprised and impressed by this overall picture of the educational qualifications of the MK taxi drivers and at first surmised that it might be something to do with the specific characteristics of the famously go-ahead Milton Keynes. But I discovered when I looked more comparatively both in the UK and abroad that the situation here was far from unparalleled. Taxi drivers may be a diverse and randomly qualified lot, but in general, and perhaps surprisingly, they are certainly *not,* as so often unthinkingly pictured, 'ignorant'.

Bottom of the heap, in sink jobs

Nor are they all poor. Admittedly some local taxi drivers, depending in what hours they work, do not make a large income from their driving as such. But some earn well. London cabbies get more take home pay per week than those in the provinces, justified, they say, by the time and expense of gaining their 'knowledge' badge, but everywhere drivers are able to increase their earnings by working longer hours.

In addition the flexibility of taxi drivers' hours, within their own control, together with – in Milton Keynes and similar cities – the typical immigrants' tradition of hard work meant that many had additional jobs. Indeed for some it was the taxi industry rather than their other job that was the sideline.

Quite a number were well off in their own right too. They had built up investments from earlier jobs for example or belonged to a family that had become wealthy in Britain or their original homeland.

Muhammad was one example. As well as driving a taxi, he was the owner of two restaurants. His father, with whom he had originally jointly owned them, was now dead so he was now managing them on his own. It meant long hours on top of driving, he said, but, like his father, he had always worked for himself and he loved it. As he kept emphasising, both he and his father (his 19-year old son too, it emerged) had always – his phrase – 'had a strong work ethic'.

It was true, he added, that his taxi business was not as lucrative as the restaurants but he liked the freedom of working for himself and it was a good use of his car (an upmarket-looking grey Mercedes). His income must have been pretty good. In the previous year he had been able to pay for his university-bound son's (inevitably costly) driving lessons and his insurance of £2500 ('no sweat' he said) and was not concerned about the high university costs to come.

Then there was Sheila, now contentedly on her third partner, who had previously run a taxi firm which she had named after her mother, and George, from Greece. He had worked for twenty years in a senior role in a travel agency. He decided to try his hand in Britain, but having found that the travel industry had at that time no openings for a foreigner, he had turned to taxi driving. Now 60 he was planning to retire soon and 'do nothing'. With his savings and a good pension from his previous jobs he had no money worries. Again there was the well-dressed and handsome driver from Ethiopia with a name meaning 'Prince' – he looked it too!

He explained that the name was fitting as he belonged to the same family as the famous Emperor Haile Selassie whom his grandfather knew well. He himself had owned super-markets in Ethiopia, then, later, in South Africa, but found this line of business did not pay well in the UK so was currently managing a suite of drivers for the Hermes delivery firm. He himself preferred taxi work as both paying better and leaving him more freedom to be with his family – also (he grinned) 'driving a taxi you don't have to get out in the wet to deliver parcels!'.

Perhaps the most striking was Nazir, an elegant and friendly gentleman in an up-market primrose wool suit, driving a large and clearly expensive car,. For three months every year, he explained, he enjoyed driving a taxi and meeting people. The rest of the time he always spent either in his mansion in Islamabad or, during the summer season, in his country estate there. His children were all at leading public schools, with one at an international school in Islamabad.

Clearly vastly more money then me!

And ill-disciplined rogues?

Certainly there are from time to time reports in the press, presumably well-founded, of taxi drivers attacking, defrauding or sexually harassing their passengers[27]. But in general, considering the thousands of taxi drivers operating, such reports are relatively few.

It may be true that the reputation of taxi drivers is low among outsiders. But not among themselves or demonstrated in their general, well-regulated, behaviour.

For one thing taxi drivers have to observe strict and sometimes inconvenient rules to avoid any attempt to poach each others'

passengers – which of course in one way they would like to do: getting passengers is after all where they get their money!

Minicab drivers were not allowed by the terms of their licence – or, as a result, by their operating companies – to pick up fares that had not been pre-booked. They were rigorous about this. Once, without transport, in an unfamiliar place, and desperate to get home I pleaded with a driver who had just dropped off a passenger to take me but – his car empty – he was adamant. Very occasionally, I was told, a driver would let you phone to his operator and book him on the spot but that was not approved as it messed up the normal order, and it very seldom happened.

It is also taboo to pick up the wrong passenger i.e. not the one who had booked the trip – even though that was something that can easily happen, especially in the crowded city centre when there can be a whole procession of booked taxis arriving. Minicab drivers do not take the first person in the queue but insist – insist – on checking the name to identify the one who had made the booking. And if that occasionally goes wrong it is by a mis-understanding (perhaps, as once happened to me, an unrecognisable pronunciation of the name), not deliberate.

Another way of ensuring the correct match is through a text sent to the prospective passenger's mobile phone detailing the car's make (not that that ever meant much to me or possibly many others), colour, and number, and sometimes the driver's name.

---

27 These are specially reported of Uber drivers, on or off duty – not, I would guess, that they are more prone to offend than other people, just that Uber drivers, being the newcomers in the situation, are somehow always newsworthy; similar incidents involving other taxi drivers tend to go unremarked or are reported just as committed by an individual, with no mention of his taxi connection.

There are also clear rules among the drivers licensed to wait in taxi ranks where, given the numbers often involved, one might have expected cut-throat competition; there is, as it were, a kind of self-regulating etiquette, neatly, if light-heartedly, expressed in 'The Ten Commandments of Saint Fiacre' (St Fiacre is said to be the patron saint of both taxi drivers and gardeners[28]):

I. Be thou always aware that an empty cab giveth way to a full cab.

II. If thou art empty and without punter [passenger] and another driver also empty permitteth thee to enter a street in front of thee, thou shalt not take the next job on that street but leave it for that driver.

III. Similarly if thou art setting down and by so doing thou dost block the path of an empty car behind thee, take thee not the next job but rather leave it to the man whom thou has hindered.

IV. Yea even though it be kipper season and then after long time jobless thou shalt not overtake a full cab.

V. If thou be with punter and thou knowest the whereabouts of other punters seeking cabs thou shalt inform drivers of empty cabs in the vicinity of those punters so that these drivers may become similarly blessed.

VI. Thou shalt not set down on a moving rank nor join a rank other than at the proper place, neither shalt thou unload alongside the point cab lest thou preventeth him from getting off.

VII. Thou shalt not park thy cab on a moving rank even when thou art bursting for a pee and thy prostate be enlarged, nor to buy a present for thy girlfriend or wife or both.

VIII. Thou shalt at all times keep the rank moving and not leave a chasm between thy cab and the next by ogling false idols on page three of a newspaper, nor shalt thou stand talking to thy mate whom thou hast not seen since yesterday, since it cause the last man in the line to lie foul.

IX. Thou shalt not broom an unwanted fare unto the driver behind thee but rather thou shouldst smile sweetly at the punter and take the job, yeah even though It be south of the river.

X. Thou shalt not pick up a street fare within an hundred cubits of a loaded rank but shouldst instead direct the punter towards the rank and the drivers thereon shall bless the warmly. (from Gates 2011: 29-30)

I met one occasion when this was broken and the second not the first driver in the queue outside the Milton Keynes railway station got the job. The reason (amusing to all but

---

28 From about 1650, the Hotel de Saint Fiacre in the rue St-Martin in Paris hired out carriages which came to be known as fiacres, thence becoming a generic term for hired horse-drawn transport (although claimed by taxi-drivers as a patron saint, St. Fiacre is not in fact recognised as such by the Catholic Church).

the driver concerned) was that when I opened the door of the expensive looking gleaming black vehicle first in the line and climbed into the back seat, the driver courteously came round to close the door for me.

The door fell off onto the ground! 'My god!'

The other taxi drivers clustered round to try to help put it back – without success. The driver next in the line helped me out, laughing, and, appropriately, ushered me into his cab.

In general, apart from some mutual criticism, drivers respect each other, the accepted conventions are followed and the system works.

And the passengers?

Truth be told it is the passengers that are more often the rogues.

There are some explicit rules to try to control passengers. By law there must be no smoking, passengers, including children, must wear seat belts, and drivers can refuse to carry certain things that pose danger. And drivers hope, sometimes explicitly insist, that passengers do not eat and drink in the cab, leave no litter or do not behave indecently. Telling a driver to drive faster and 'back seat driving' when passengers try to tell the fully knowledgeable driver the way is not illegal, but much resented.

In sum, there seems to be a kind of implicit contract between passengers and drivers, as well as other road users, by which each are confidently expected to behave with decency and good sense.

The drunks are another thing again. Many drivers prefer not to pick them up at all, but it can be difficult to refuse – ' 'Oh no!' I say when I see one coming, but what can you do?'. Most drivers just tolerate them as part of the job. After all everyone agrees that it is better for drunks to be in a taxi rather than driving themselves home – an important, widely

accepted, role of taxis[30]. The exception of course is if they are too drunk to remember where they are going or where they live.

But there is no real protection against the main problem most often posed by passengers. This is seldom violence or attempts at outright robbery, though these do no doubt sometimes occur. What drivers suffer regularly from is passengers 'bilking' or 'doing a runner': reaching the end of the taxi journey then simply walking off without paying.

Almost all the drivers I asked had encountered at least some examples; for one it was happening. 'about twice a week'. To the question of what kind of people were most likely to do this the answer (to me surprising, I'd expected it to be rough young men and drunks) was 'young teenage girls'.

It seems drivers are helpless to counteract this. Even if a policeman is prepared to come in answer to a call – improbable – they are unlikely to take action. And taking action themselves is not on – as one driver said 'How would people react, do you think, if they saw a black man running after a young girl in the street however justified he claimed to be'. So they just shrug and absorb it as part of being a taxi driver.

They do however also have some good stories of getting their own back and thwarting the miscreants. One choice example was of a very drunk young man getting into a taxi for a long drive at midnight, likely to cost £100 or more. Reaching his destination he reached for the door, got out and staggered rapidly away, laughing: 'So you thought I'd pay you, did

---

[30] In countries like Finland where by law there is zero alcohol tolerance for drivers taxis especially flourish.

you, ha ha ha!' The joke was on him, however. As the driver recounted with delight, the bilker hadn't noticed that his wallet had fallen out of his pocket and was lying on the back seat.

Ruffians or carers?

'Taxi drivers are the only profession that is truly united – we all hate the public!'

They may make a joke of it and maybe in abstract terms there is something in sayings like these; there are two sides to the transaction after all and they don't have to be fond of each other. But in practice helpfulness and consideration are part of the requirements of the job and in terms of actual experience – and I have been driven by hundreds – I have seldom (except in New York) met with anything but kindness and consideration. Most pride themselves on taking care of their customers and I myself would say that taxi drivers overall really do deserve the sobriquet of 'knights of the road'.

They are prepared to come round and gently open the door and help me out of the car if I seem to need it. And if I say 'Sorry to be so slow' as I struggle out they'll be sure to respond with something like 'There's no hurry' or 'Don't rush my darling' (a term they use with respect) or, in courteous tones, 'Don't worry, I think you're like my grandmother'. Sometimes they reverse the car down our narrow awkward drive to let me out right at the door, or carry my bags down the drive for me without expecting thanks.

Their usual rule is that they don't go *into* a customer's house. That makes good sense. As one put it, 'I drive a lot of women and what if a husband comes back and sees me there? I did once go in and help a passenger hang her curtains, they were too high for her to reach, then I got out quick'. There are of course exceptions and not every driver is kind on every occasion. There was the driver, already

paid by the hospital, who insisted on the patient paying again, was surly throughout, and, worst, refused to drive him (very frail) up to his door, which had been perfectly feasible for other drivers,

Among my many journeys I had just a few bad experiences (drivers after all are all too human)

In the first, I vividly remember Matthew, who, unusually among taxi drivers, was UK born and well known among other drivers for his discourtesy (the firm eventually was sensible enough put him on the regular prison run). As well as being rude and grumpy all through the journey, he wouldn't drive me right up to the easily accessible door and despite my heavy bag refused to help me with it. On top of that he declined to give me a receipt, saying that 'It's not my car' (untrue as I later discovered and irrelevant anyway), 'I'm not allowed to', which was nonsense. I tried to insist since it was one of the few occasions when with a receipt I could reclaim my taxi fare as expenses, but no good, I gave up.

Actually I had had an earlier experience with him too. One afternoon, due home soon and therefore choosing a taxi rather than a bus as (I thought) quicker, I waited and waited at the agreed place, then finally saw what looked like my taxi draw up some distance away. I waved frantically but saw him drive off. I contacted the booking company who reported that he had said I hadn't been there. I re-ordered and waited another 20 minutes when he finally came back. 'Why didn't you wait?' I remonstrated 'or phone me that you were there?' (something taxi drivers regularly did if they couldn't immediately spot their passenger) 'Oh I could have done a lot of things but why should I?' What a grump!''

The other really bad example was not of driver discourtesy – far from it – but of the task just not being carried out as expected. I needed to get to Oxford, usually an hour's journey, for an urgent appointment. I allowed extra time when I booked and cleared in advance that I could pay with a card. First, she was 15 minutes late arriving. Then, despite my protests, she detoured lengthily to buy petrol (the unwritten understanding is that drivers *never* do this once they've picked up their fare). Then she claimed her satnav wasn't working and she would have to 'quickly' (it took 20 minutes!) 'pop home' for a replacement. I protested, but, locked in the taxi, as it were, could do nothing. Predictably we arrived nearly an hour late. Then she refused to accept a card – 'not allowed' (not true). After an argument she grudgingly processed it. It took another 15 minutes.

Mind you, her manners were charming. But I resisted her suggestion to book her for my return journey. The taxi company – to whom one can always complain – apologised and said she had been 'spoken to, it will not happen again'. She continued with them however and I did not, as I had fleetingly hoped, get a refund. An expensive day.

Those experiences were horrid but in a way the exceptions proved the rule and other drivers to whom I recounted these experiences seemed genuinely shocked. These occasions did in fact bring home to me how polite and helpful by far the majority of taxi drivers are, matched by my and other passengers' expectations that they will indeed be so – a kind of implicit bargain.

'If I wake up feeling in a bad mood', said one 'or everything has gone wrong, but then I do something to help a passenger, I feel good for the rest of the day'.

KNOWING
AND BEING

Chapter 7: Knowing the ways and ways of knowing

Once told the destination, taxi drivers are expected to know how to get there without any further direction. They are assumed just to *know*. *And they do.*

London taxi drivers are especially famous for their knowledge and rightly so. They look down on younger drivers who haven't been through a similar course or even – horror! – depend on the satellite navigation (satnavs) now installed in many vehicles or available through the driver's iPhone.

© Duncan Cuthbertson | Dreamstime.com

Aerial view of Milton Keynes roads, the names of which the taxi driver must know in detail.

Older, experienced drivers claim, probably justifiably for the most part, that they rely on their own knowledge and that they only use satnavs when they have a job that takes them further afield, outside their known area. This is especially true of London hackney drivers, who understandably pride themselves on their expert knowledge. So becoming a taxi driver is not just knowing how to drive a car, be courteous, and have good eyesight. A lot more knowledge is needed.'

What is 'the knowledge' and how drivers get it?

> *'It's like a scar, the knowledge.*
> *It never leaves you'.*

So said a London cabbie. And not surprisingly since the famous 'knowledge' of London black cab drivers is so extensive and detailed that it has been claimed that it even alters the physical format of their brains. What's more it is widely taken as *the* ultimate characteristic of 'The Taxi Driver'. Everywhere, until relying on satnavs was in some places allowed to partially replace it, being a taxi driver has entailed comprehensive knowledge of all features of the local area. For as well as all the other requirements, they have to pass a rigorous and fearsome test of their knowledge of the locality that goes right down to the smallest detail. The famous 'knowledge' of London black cab drivers is, as I say, the best known and the best documented. It is looked up to by all drivers as the hardest to obtain, the pinnacle, it would seem, of knowledge.

Paul Vlaar: http://www.neep.net/photofjapan/

Taxi ride through Kyoto, GPS navigation system installed

It takes many years and a great deal of money to acquire this knowledge for not only are there the rigours of the test but the lengthy

Panoramic taxi ride round London (Garner and Stokoe, 2000

"Travellers' Club to Kensington Manor Hotel? Pall Mall to Emperor's Gate, sir. Leave on the left Pall Mall. Right St James's Street. Left Piccadilly. Comply Hyde Park Corner. Leave by Knightsbridge. Bear left Brompton Road. Bear right Thurlowe Place. Forward Cromwell Gardens. Forward Cromwell Road. Left and right Stanhope Gardens. Right Gloucester Road. Left Southwell Gardens. Left Grenville Place. Right Emperor's Gate. Set down on right."

time, typically three years, sometimes more, that it takes working for it, full time. Candidates give up their jobs in order to focus on learning the ways so that the cost of getting the knowledge, given the loss of earnings while studying for the test, is commonly said to be around £20,000 in London, somewhat less in the provinces.

Drivers have a variety of tried and tested ways of learning and of remembering, and individuals choose the ones(s) that best suit their circumstances and personality.

Practical, fast, and on-the-spot knowledge is essential. Aspirants can only fully get this by travelling along the routes and runs, and by visiting the points personally. They need to observe and remember not just the street names and characteristics but anything else that the passenger might want, like interesting buildings, museums, galleries, pubs, well-known shops, cemeteries … and new streets and developments as well as old. They need to know not just navigation but the detail of the drive-round panoramas some passengers want, together with the history and anecdotes and witticisms that go with them.

It is not just streets, incredibly numerous as they are, but other – that is, all – places of interest. They need to know their locations, and the route(s) to reach them, including: Streets of any kind (main, alleys, squares, closes, parades … etc etc)

- Financial and commercial centres
- Places of worship
- Sport stadiums and leisure centres
- Museums and art galleries
- Palaces and other notable stately dwellings
- Civil, criminal and coroners' courts
- Housing estates
- Diplomatic premises
- Hotels
- Clubs and restaurants
- Prisons
- Parks and open spaces
- Town halls
- Hospitals
- Theatres and cinemas
- Schools, colleges and universities
- Places of interest to tourists
- Government offices and Departments
- Registry Offices
- Cemeteries
- Bus, underground and rail stations
- Police stations
- Banks and company headquarters buildings
- Associations and institutions

Indeed they need to know, and at once, any place, street or road in London where a passenger might ask to be taken, together with recent events such as closed roads, temporary one-way streets, accidents or extra traffic that might affect the normal, memorised, route. It seems impossible that any one man or woman

could master and retain all that knowledge and answer to it in a fast oral test. And yet – human ingenuity and commitment … they do.

No wonder London black cab drivers while on the one hand thought of as anonymous quasi-automations, have at the same time a reputation for near-superhuman mental powers of knowledge. Just one partial example of an answer that might be required in a London Knowledge Test (Garner and Stokoe 2000)

Maps: good source for the knowledge of places
(Garner and Stokoe 2000)

The effort is clearly regarded as worth it: hundreds apply each year in the hope, as it is confidently expressed by one of their number of 'joining an elite club of the world's most respected taxi drivers' (Anon 2013).

A taxi drivers' training school opened in 1927 and there is now a flourishing industry to assist in the acquiring of this knowledge – self-learning instruction books, manuals, legal guides, maps, college courses, face to face and online 'knowledge schools' costing, at one point, around £40 a month.

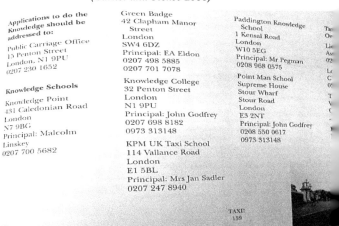

In addition to the practical riding around, the average student does 15 to 30 hours a week study for three years. And then, if they pass, they are proudly qualified black cabbies: 'butterboys'.

And more knowledge …

Outside London it is easier for aspirant drivers to acquire the necessary knowledge but it still involves an immense amount of meticulous memorising. The areas covered are, it is true, smaller than London but still often extensive (Birmingham, for instance, Belfast, Glasgow).

A Buttery's Guide to Cab Etiquette

Now that you are blessed with the coveted green badge and will henceforth be known as *'one who thinks he owns the bloody road'*, it is time to let you in to the secrets of your chosen profession – the unwritten rules or 'Ten Commandments', which novice taxi drivers would do well to follow. I mean cab *etiquette* – yes, there is such a thing! Without it there would be anarchy on our streets. Let's leave that that to minicabs – and bendy-buses and behave instead in a manner befitting our proud traditions of nearly 400 years.

Be proud and keep to the rules … (Gates 2011)

In ever growing cities like Milton Keynes the grid layout may help but there are likely to be, daily, new estates, streets, schools, and more to learn. Passengers won't be happy with 'It's new, I don't know'. The whole point of taxi drivers from the passengers' point of view is that they *do* know, whatever the unusual request.

Akeel in Milton Keynes, for example, had, among other things, to keep up his expert knowledge of the changing locations of brothels. He was often called to drive young girls – prostitutes – and their clients. As he explained, 'there are, of course, 'no street walkers or brothels in Milton Keynes', er, just a number of 'single girl apartments', what's illegal about that?' He needed to know where they were. A well known one (now closed) had been in Bletchley, but there were others 'all over the city centre, the biggest, upmarket, one run by Lithuanians'.

So the tests – and the constant updating – have to be taken seriously and studied hard for by whatever method proved feasible best for the individual aspirant.

They had, then, to have a comprehensive knowledge of the roads generally also covers driver and vehicle conditions, the Highway Code, road signs, comprehension, customer care and points of interest. The applicant must also have held an official driving licence for 12 months, a current UK visa for at least 18 months, and a satisfactory medical certificate and have no criminal record. Pretty comprehensive![31]

Tests arranged by the local council were described as tense but once you got down to it and, provided you were well prepared, do-able. Drivers described their experience of local tests: 'Eight of us were sat round a table, you were given a set amount of time to answer a series of questions; we had to get a high proportion right to pass; I was lucky and passed first time – it wasn't so bad – but two didn't. They'd probably learn a bit more and try again'. In another account it was twenty questions, later lowered to ten of which you had to get seven right.

In addition to this all-aspirant taxi drivers had to satisfy other requirements such as advanced driving competence, knowledge of the national Highway Code, basic maintenance, courtesy, and absence of any criminal record. In addition their car must be roadworthy and no more than three years old. Then there might be further tests and training carried out by the particular taxi firm(s) with whom they decided to sign up.

If successful they got a 'plate' qualifying them as local cabdrivers, a valuable and essential requirement.

Some drivers came from taxi driving families and had been absorbing the necessary knowledge from the outset. Others had started as delivery boys, despatch riders, bus drivers or the like, gradually developing their knowledge of the streets in that way, then realising they could build on this to qualify as taxi drivers. Now fully fledged as taxi drivers, they in a way seemed to feel that this had always been their natural destiny.

Peter for example, now a longtime London taxi driver, had left school at 15 ('a duffer', he said) to become a bricklayer but after five years had thought – clearly *not* a duffer! – about taking up taxi driving.

---

[31] Given its value, one might wonder whether there, as in many fields, there are ways around the official requirements. In Milton Keynes in the past it seems, from the detailed account quoted earlier, that there may have been. But drivers were near-unanimous in saying that the current processes are clean and that it was to everyone's interest, including their own, to keep it so.

He set to and after working at it for the usual three years, succeeded in passing the black cab Knowledge test. Now a fully-fledged cabbie he was earning enough to keep his family and 'on the whole, I like it'.

Converted taxi as fire fighter in the 1939-45 war
(Eales c2005)

The knowledge needed by a taxi driver goes beyond just a mastery of location, for taxi drivers are and have been utilised for many purposes – for transporting goods as well as people, for sight seeing, hospital tasks, even'(as in the war) fire-fighting.

There can be carrying out detective work too, being a local historian, penetrating and rescuing from a danger zone, and much else. Drivers must know too how to deal with passengers in various physical and emotional states – not just calm and well but ill, wounded, bereaved, angry, hysterical, drunk, amorous, lost, and so on and so on.

That too (Hodges 2007)

For their own sakes too, drivers also need to be able to judge passengers' trustworthiness: are they likely to pay or to abscond? (an important aspect well brought out in Gambetta and Hamill's analysis, 2005). The tests try to assess an aspirant's overall potential, but they cannot cover everything.

Getting to the right place

Once told a destination, taxi drivers are expected to know how to reach it without any further direction.

To the passenger sitting comfortably inside this may seem a simple matter, and perhaps sometimes it is. At any rate it is not *their* concern. But for the driver – just consider the maze of streets in any urban area.

Even in relatively straightforward Milton Keynes the knowledge needed is enormous.And even when the streets and buildings are known, and the best routes to get there, the driver has to be alertly observant to somehow identify house numbers – quite often obscure or missing – in order to land the passengers on the right side of the street and at exactly the right number – and that however dark or rainy it is. The passenger just assumes all will be well and in fact, though there are sometimes misunderstandings about the location of *pick-up* location, there seem to be remarkably few mistakes about the final destinations. The passengers, as I say, sit back, relaxed and confident they are in the hands of experts – which, of course, they are.

There are of course many ways to conceptualise 'place'[32]: as a fixed spot on a map; a planner's projection; a point with location but no magnitude as in geometry; a resounding name; a measured monetary distance; geographical destination; multi-sensory experience; the shifting, elusive space of dreams.

---

[32] See for example the contrasting papers in Majevadia 2,016.

Doubtless one or more of these are shared by one driver or another, perhaps as an unthought background in keeping with their personal experience and the perceived objectives of the expected test. For practical purposes however learners are likely to focus on the idea of a fixed geographical location on a map. They will think little about complex abstract complexities of potential interest to the analyst, but rather, realistically, focus on infallibly memorising the questions they are likely to be faced with: the routes to reach given spots.

Drivers have a variety of tried and tested ways of learning and of remembering these. Best known is the preparation for the famous London black cab drivers test, looked up to, as I say, by all drivers, many passengers and general opinion too, the pinnacle, it would seem, of knowledge.

Preparing for it takes a great deal of money – an investment, drivers would say, for not only are there the rigours of the test itself but the lengthy time, typically three or more years and often without income, that it takes working for it. Candidates often gave up their jobs in order to focus full-time on learning the ways. This meant that, as I was often told, getting the knowledge, including loss of earnings while studying for the test, commonly came to around £20,000 in London, somewhat less in the provinces.

By now there are multiple aids to help them acquire the necessary knowledge: colleges specially set up for this purpose with both face to face and distant courses[33]. There are also books; practice papers; maps; audio instruction; and advice to engage joint learning and testing with a buddy (often considered the best method to supplement and reinforce your learning).

The test itself, whether in London or elsewhere, traditionally included not only a comprehensive knowledge of the roads

generally but also driver personal details, vehicle conditions, the Highway Code, road signs, comprehension, customer care and points of interest. The applicant must also have held an official driving licence for 12 months, a current UK visa for at least 18 months, and a satisfactory medical certificate, and have no criminal record – pretty comprehensive!

For the established test, prospective drivers must instantly know the location of at least all the principal landmarks and how to get there: among them the stations, the churches. schools, libraries, hospital, health centres, and tourist attractions.

Bletchley Park, home of the WW2 code breakers – one of the principal Milton Keynes points of interest

Peace Pagoda at Willen Lake, North

For Milton Keynes the traditional drivers' test would have covered not just the location and routes to every major and minor street and

---

[33] Many listed at london.taxi.knowledge.colleges/

housing complex but also, among other things, stations, pubs, schools, colleges, banks, supermarkets, parks and medical centres as well as landmarks like Bletchley Park, home of the famous Second World War Enigma codebreakers, the 'Peace Pagoda', and the 'Tree Cathedral' (Photo on Page 31).

The further testing of course comes in the day-to-day actual driving of passengers, for drivers must be sure to know of any current traffic jams, detours, road closures and, however temporary, one-way streets, speed restrictions and road repair obstacles. Some drivers also know, or are expected to know, useful details like the main train timetable, shop, museum and sports centre opening times and entry requirements – not that these are parts of the formal test.

By now the burden of updating on local and temporary conditions and memorising roads etc is much eased by the availability of satnav navigation. Specially for local minicab drivers (but not the London black cabbies) the sheer memorising aspect test itself has in very recent years been in this way much lightened making getting into the taxi industry a much easier prospect. Experienced drivers however still pride themselves on needing satnavs only as a backup if at all, and take pride in their active and demonstrable local knowledge of the ways of their area.

Memory strategies and how to know

How do drivers remember in this remarkable way?

Which resources they primarily relied on for learning and activating this knowledge seemed to be largely a matter of individual choice and personality. It is interesting to relate their strategies to more general accounts of memory.

One classic account is Frederick Bartlett's *Memory* (1932). This suggests that remembering is not, as we sometimes picture it, a purely intellectual computer-like matter

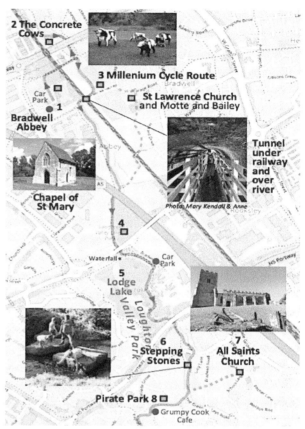

Some famous but hidden places in Milton Keynes
(Extract from the Pilgrim Trail Map, Milton Keynes)

of information processing, but rather a more personal creative process of reconstructing memories more imaginatively, relating them to personal associations and experiences. Remembering, in other words, is not a kind of tape recorder or video that somehow faithfully plays back our experiences but something rooted in more personal schemas, moulded by, and fitting into, our individual experiences.

There are also the memory processes of other times and places. One rightly famous account is Mary Carruthers' description (2000) of how people in the ancient and mediaeval worlds constructed memories. Their methods were essentially based on *visual* recollection independent of the *written* forms we might rely on now – at that time reliance on the writing, let alone written memos, was in any case sparse compared to now, and maps, where they were available at all, less a plan of routes than statements of religious cosmology – and at a global rather than local level.

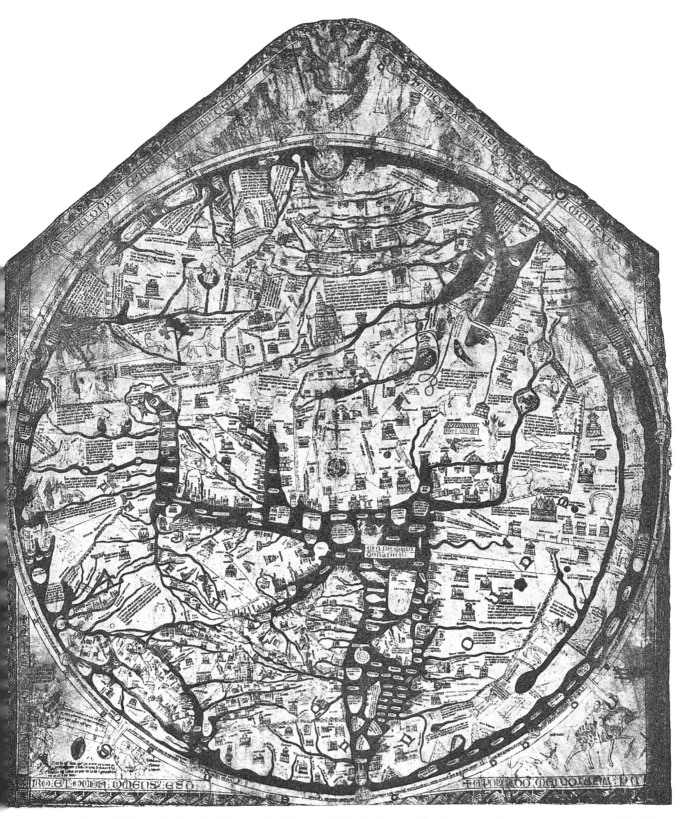

This 'Pictorial Map' is housed in Hereford Cathedral and is one of Britain's finest medieval treasures. Great world maps were an English speciality in the Middle Ages and were drawn on cloth, walls or animal skin. Only this, the Hereford World Map – Mappa Mundi – has survived complete and is believed to be the world's largest medieval map.

These large maps were drawn and illustrated in great detail. As pictorial descriptions of the outside world, these impressive maps were also educational; they were used for teaching geography, natural history and classical legends.

The way this ancient memory method worked was in one way quite simple. It was based on the visual associations you can create as you move along your memory's way. The idea was to picture yourself going into a room and seeing the content there: perhaps a vase, a chair, a statuette. Each thing you passed you would associate with one of the things you wished to remember making them easy to recall (we know that ancient and mediaeval cultures were deeply auditory but can see from their memory strategies that they were highly visual too).

And now? What about the specific case of taxi drivers' remarkable memorising, covering a scope of information astounding to the rest of us?

Well, almost every day I was in touch with taxi drivers – people who specialised in memory processing. So, as I sat in the front seat, questioning, I found it interesting to ask them about their ways of remembering.

I was curious about how in the first place they had *acquired* their knowledge, and, then, afterwards, *retained and used* it. Some thought these odd questions since it concerned a process too well-known to need comment, but most found them quite interesting to reflect on. For London drivers in particular it had likely been their main preoccupation for several years, one too that had taken them out of full–time paid employment for a substantial period. For local drivers too, except for the most recent (satnav-assisted) aspirants who had admittedly been less challenged, it had also been a serious commitment.

Modern taxi drivers, it seems, use a variety of strategies for remembering. These vary according to their personalities and backgrounds and, seemingly unlike earlier memorisers[34], different *individuals* do it different ways.

Setting out to learn the roads (Warren 2003)

The commonest method is to buy or borrow a moped or small motorcycle (in earlier years a pedal bike) and set off on it either alone or in a group to explore and memorise the streets and main locations by going round seeing them on the ground; 'there's something about the actual close feel and touch of the street that fixes it in a way going by car never does'.

All those places – it can take years, no wonder some give up in despair.

They often start with some easy standard route, for example from one main railway station such as Euston to another main station, say Victoria. Once that is mastered, then they learn other branching roots going out from there in a circle around it, consolidating in, say, eight or so major routes. Then, building on that, they take other starting points and other destinations – and so on and so on until the incredible number of streets, almost too many for an outsider to take in, let alone recall in detail.

Ideally they learn and remember through personal physical sightings – always

---

[34] Or perhaps not – as so often for earlier history we know about the common patterns but not the possible individual variations.

significant – but they cannot be everywhere and other aids like maps are essential.

And then, allied to other cues and, since remembering is not just an intellectual process, personal associations, there is also, maybe not fully conscious, the *feel* as well as the sight of the streets, the remembered, felt, experience of steering to left or right in traffic lanes, the flow of the traffic, intensified in due course by the enjoyed skill behind the wheel, taking advantage of the best routes not only across a city but within a particular road. The familiar patterns (schemas) of intersections and networks and branching routes, linked together in a wider structure, may come in as something more – almost in a sense poetic – than just an isolated piece of mechanical information.

The ancient and mediaeval system of *visual* cues as well as Bartlett's emphasis on personal associations would seem still to apply to modern taxi drivers' learning and remembering. They draw on both the *visual* pictures associated with travelling along local streets and past famous buildings and their (somewhat different) use of visual maps; *and* on the method of starting from one standard route, set in, and coloured by, the context of their personal experience, then extended out to other routes.

The taxi drivers I spoke with seemed to use a range of strategies for calling up their remembered knowledge. These varied according to their personalities and their cultural and educational backgrounds and, seemingly unlike earlier memorisers, different *individuals* do it different ways.

Some learned and remembered best in auditory mode. There was the driver for instance that explained that 'You say it over and over to yourself in your mind; you can feel it in your inner ear, and then you get to know it so now I have it when somebody asks me to go somewhere'. This auditory

remembering could be reinforced by learning through personal vocalised repetitions aloud (that is what would work best for me as it happens), audio recordings, and – said probably to be the most effective method – face to face vocal interchange with a co-learner.

For some, learning is basically a matter of orientation – north, south etc – plotted onto a map of the whole area, eventually all in your head.

And then for the walkers or riders there is no doubt that, allied to other cues and not fully conscious, there was the *felt* experience of driving on the streets, the familiar remembered feel of steering to left or right in traffic lanes, the flow of the traffic, all perhaps intensified in due course by the enjoyed skill behind the wheel, taking advantage of the best routes not only across a city but within a particular road. The majority however seemed in one way or another to rely on *visual* cues for both learning and remembering.

When asked about what they thought when a particular destination was requested, many said it was the *look* of the place they were going to, the sight of the street and building names, and the places they pass: the full route stood there in their mind. For others it came to them in instalments as they went.

Ideally their knowledge came through personal sightings but learners could not be everywhere and *maps* too were found essential.

Map memory was a basic foundation for very many of them. Some had maps of the local area on their walls at home, or kept one or more in their cars, constantly refreshing their memories during breaks. For another, it was a vivid *image*, 'It is as if in a helicopter looking down on the city from above, seeing the routes'.

Chapter 8: Sharing and shared, taxi drivers knowledge

Taxi drivers know many things, some in common with the rest of us, some specific to their profession. They know their own stories and how they got to be here, and their families and their background and (often) many languages. They know the locations where they work. They have learned the knowledge they need to be taxi drivers. They know where they are.

They learn from their passengers too and from each other. There is all the knowledge surrounding taxi drivers, learned and shared in the liminal space within those enclosing car doors, and in the conversations, shared sayings, and literature about and around taxi drivers. And there is their own knowledge too, whether hidden (even from themselves) or articulated, as for all of us, of their own, enduring, selves,

Well, you learn ...

'Imagination carries us to world that never was, but without it we go nowhere'

Taxi drivers' knowledge, in other words, is not just about how to drive or where to find places. There is much much more.

Let us remember the intimate, temporary space that they share with their passengers. Individuals tend to open up in this liminal setting of even a short taxi ride. It does not happen on every occasion of course but there is commonly something special in being in an enclosed, intimate space with someone who is both initially and eventually, a stranger, someone to whom you will have no on-going commitments and who is thus somehow a-social, not quite a person, so safe to open up to – yet at the same time also a kind of confidential trusted listener, outside the conventions and expectations of, as it were, 'normal' life.

The driver can pretty safely be assumed to be someone they will never meet again or at any rate not be recognised as a confidant. It can be between co-passengers too. The intimacy of the circumscribed time-limited taxied journey together may lead to all kinds of confidences: the start or development of a love affair, the beginning of a story, the initiation of an academic companionship, as for me, once, in the brief intensity of a taxi ride. In this setting it feels safe to share knowledge, the details never to be divulged to others: of marital problems, secret love affairs, fears, dreams, drugs, emprisonment, money issues, corrupt stratagems, manipulating the system through 'ways around', difficult people and how to cope with them, or the problems and delights of older people 'like my granny'.

Above all it is from passenger to driver. This is not just something dreamt up from the observer's imagination, but evinced in taxi drivers' frequent descriptions of themselves as 'the agony aunts of the streets' – half joking but serious too.

It is also taken seriously by governmental and charity urbanisations. Here is the Suicide Prevention Bristol's 'Not the Last Stop' encouragement to taxi drivers to be aware of the signs that could indicate someone was contemplating taking their own life.

'We are encouraging them [taxi drivers] if they believe there is an immediate risk to their passenger's life or they are in danger, to flag it up on their system so emergency services can be called ...Also we just want to encourage the taxi drivers to start up a conversation if it is a lone passenger who they believe are in danger'.

Taxi drivers are well aware of this role. It is something akin to that of a priest or a confidential therapist – a listener.

The shared wisdoms of drivers

So there is much to learn about and from taxi drivers, that relates to what they in turn learn from, and share with, their passengers.

Some of it of course is just the practical down-to-earth, but sometimes important, knowledge that can be learnt from drivers. A common saying is 'Call a taxi! Ask a driver!'

And it is true. There is widely shared belief that if you want to know what is really going on somewhere, the best thing to do is to go there, get a taxi, and ask the driver. This is evidenced year after year. We see it even from the most high-powered of visiting journalists when, relying among other things on their taxi driver sources, they report authoritatively about some situation as 'our foreign correspondent'.

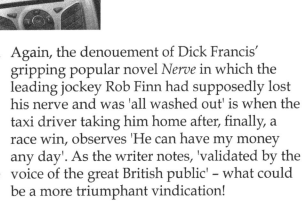

They are justified too, for taxi drivers drive all manner of people, and do so every day, through even the most complex and controversial situations, with their eyes and their ears necessarily open to the events, experiences and conflicting voices they encounter. They have to know what is going in, what areas are closed, where there might be problems, how they can get to where they need to go. They have in a way a kind of free pass to everywhere around, their 'Taxi' sign a kind of white pass of neutrality guaranteeing safe passage and return.

On something of the same lines they are widely regarded as in some symbolic sense the voice of public opinion. When just the other day a government minister was talking about a controversial new tax, the test for him was clearly not how it would go down with the politicians or the elite, but, he said, how he would 'justify it to the Bangladeshi taxi drivers in Riverside, where I live'[36]: taxi drivers taken as signifyimg 'the common man'.

Again, the denouement of Dick Francis' gripping popular novel *Nerve* in which the leading jockey Rob Finn had supposedly lost his nerve and was 'all washed out' is when the taxi driver taking him home after, finally, a race win, observes 'He can have my money any day'. As the writer notes, 'validated by the voice of the great British public' – what could be a more triumphant vindication!

There is also a wealth of shared knowledge about and around taxis which the drivers too imbibe and pass on. As one put it of this kind of knowledge, 'Well, you learn …'. Whether or not they *explicitly* know the many taxi-related sayings, the context in which they arise and the general atmosphere they implicitly create, without doubt in subtle ways affect drivers' lives and outlook.

---

[36] BBC website July 21 2022.

Among other things drivers laugh at them-selves and their reputation .

I went to the taxi driver reunion. Everyone turned up half an hour late.

A book on taxi drivers? That's like a book on wild animals in the zoo only here they're out of their cages.

They take their experiences seriously too – their pains and joys, their lives as part of the down-to-earth wit and, in a way, glory, of life today. Some are straight jokes or – highly popular among both drivers and passengers – puns.

No matter how many times I visit this city, I'm always struck by the same thing: a yellow taxi cab.

What's worse for traffic than when it's foggy? When it's hailing taxis.

Heard a great new band called 'Taxi'. They are tipped to go all the way.

My friend always went the extra mile at work. That's why he lost his job as a taxi driver.

I love this up to the minute:

Someone jumped in my taxi, pointed to a chap in front and shouted 'Follow him'. I said, 'Sure, what's his twitter handle?'

And the many versions of:

A chap jumps in a taxi and says, 'King Arthur's Close'. The taxi driver says, 'Don't worry I'll lose him at the lights'.

Jokey sayings can also be ways of coping with the racist or derogatory attitudes that taxi drivers are aware of among some passengers:

They think I ride an elephant at home!

It's not how you look, it's what you do, innit.

Journeys, taxi driven or other, are commonly used as metaphors about wider issues, encapsulating in a way the wisdom of many generations:

The only way to get to the end of the journey is to travel the road that leads to it. And, a journey of 1000 miles starts with a single step.

It is worth delving into the deep truth, as it would seem to be, of the shared 'knowledge', wit and insight derived from and relating to taxis and taxi drivers as drivers and passengers communicate knowledge between each other.

Taxi drivers are in fact a notable conduit for the wisdom and sayings of generations as they hear and pass on the familiar and unfamiliar insights they gather from their many passengers.

It is not of course only their own first hand beliefs but also the sayings they hear from their passengers and go on to share – a notable conduit indeed.

Like the much quoted but still vibrant sayings such as: *a true friend is one who knows the song in your heart and can sing it back to you when you forgotten the words – Love is blind, but the neighbours ain't! – behind every great man is a woman rolling her eyes.*

The taxi – the world

Beyond that, taxi journeys and taxi drivers are used for metaphorical commentary – a way of seeing the world, life, and our journey through it in perspective. This comes out in sayings heard and passed on by taxi drivers, such as:

- *Life is like a taxi – the meter just keeps a ticking whether you are getting somewhere or just standing still.*

- *The road to success is always under construction.*

- *If you're not listening to life it will remind you.*

- *The grass may be greener on the other side but it's just as hard to mow.*

- *Originality is unexplored territory. You get there by carrying your own canoe – you can't take a taxi.*

And on the nature and destiny of people – of human life:

- *If you think your life is bland then you haven't added enough flavour.*

- *You are the pink flamingo on the great lawn of life, be brilliant.*

- *Yesterday is history, tomorrow is a mystery, today is a gift, that's why it's called the present.*

And – fitingly enunciated by immigrant taxi drivers needing to make their way in the world.

- *Opportunity is missed by most people because it is in overalls and looks like work.*

- *The only place where success comes before work is in the dictionary.*

- *Your best helping hand is on the end of your arm.*

- *No journey is ever finished.*

The back of a taxi is commonly used as setting for the start or denouement of a story, especially a love story. In 1910 songwriters were already celebrating the romance of young love in a taxi ride.

'Taxi' sheet music
(courtesy Nancy Groce)

More highbrow literary example are Bellow's Herzog and Hemingway's The sun also rises[37]. Taxis, their drivers, and their journeys appear as a symbol, good or bad, obvious or mysterious, according to your outlook, of human life and its destiny – again , the 'life is like a taxi' image. References to taxi drivers and journeys can be used to express a kind of social comment from a perspective, looking out and in, on the places, perhaps entrapped in metaphor, that the taxi is taking you past[38].

---

[37] More examples at theguardian.com/books/2010/oct/16/ten-best-taxis literature/

[38] *London taxi drive* by the Caribbean poet David Dabydeen being a notable example.

They come in poetry and in sayings that resonate with the widely shared symbolism of life as a kind of journey undertaken in a detached and time-limited, fleeting, space, that is at the same time somehow eternal – in a taxi.

A hospital bed is a parked taxi with a meter running. (Groucho Marx)

Silence sat in the taxi, as though a stranger had got in. (Elizabeth Bowen)

She had the perpetual sense, as she watched the taxi cabs, of being out, out, far out to sea and alone; she always had the feeling that it was very, very, dangerous to live even one day. (Virginia Woolf)

At least they looked that way to me from the taxi window
and since I happened to be sitting
that fading Sunday afternoon
in the very centre of the universe. (William Taylor Collins)

Trying to make you disappear
Make ya pack your bags
Get the hell out of here
Ding-dong, the sound I'm waiting for
Your taxi's outside
And the driver's at the door. (Montell Jordan)

At the violet hour, when the eyes and back turn upward from the desk
When the human engine waits like a taxi throbbing, waiting,
I Tiresias, though blind, throbbing between two lives,
Old man with wrinkled female breasts, can see
At the violet hour, the evening hour that strives Homeward, and brings the sailor home from sea.
(T S Eliot, The Waste Land)

And so on and on through quotes and sayings, literary, humorous or profound. So much to learn, so many experiences of life and its journeys[39].

Literature can indeed bring understanding. It can envisage a taxi and its journey as a microcosm of the world, the world as the magical grain of sand in a cab's front seats. Might there also perhaps be a sense in which heaven can be found in the dreams of 'just a taxi driver's' story and his or her patient waiting?

---

[39] Further examples in Appendix 2. Perhaps unsurprisingly, there are a number of web collections of sayings about or arising from taxis, among them quotemaster.org/qa9b052110d7eea9b5cf00362a93846ca/, wisesayings.com/taxi-quotes/, inspiringquotes.us/topic/7779-taxi/, also the extensive collection in Solomon 2011.

Chapter 9: The real me

'Where am I myself, the whole man, the true man?
(Ibsen)

Even for full-time taxi drivers, life isn't just driving the roads and remembering the way, or even helping and talking to their passengers and sharing their thoughts. Their knowledge of the ways is remarkable and amazing indeed – let that never be forgotten. But there are *many* ways of knowing, many kinds of memory, many native languages and cultures besides those – themselves multiple – of Europe.

The incoming taxi drivers in Milton Keynes streets had come, like their compatriots of many lands, with culturalmemories and ways of knowing deep embedded in their reality[40]. It is not possible to follow this up in detail here, but that too is a dimension not to be forgotten, arguably a hidden structure lying behind, and adding meaning to, the everyday actions and knowledge.

There is also the reality of dream, the presence of the non-material, the meaning of their deep, own, selves.

Who am I in the universe?

So let me come me to a more intimate and personal dimension. At first sight it will seem only marginal to the study of taxi drivers. But wait. Even if in some ways it's import remains below the level of consciousness, it can also be seen to be somehow at the heart of things *This is the driver's **name**.*

When I get into the front seat of a taxi, the first thing we do is to exchange names: a common practice, and light-hearted – but with something more to it than that. As in some other personal interactions, it amounts to a kind of *gift exchange* (to use a favourite anthropological term[41]): not only an acknowledgement of, and commitment to, a kind of bargain and exchange between server and client, but a giving of oneself, a mark of personal trust.

So do names and their exchange *matter*? Let me set the subject in perspective. This needs a little comparative background[42].

Names, it turns out, are everywhere central to our selves, to our sense of self. If we want a human and personal rather than mechanical contact with someone the first thing we want to know is their name. Indeed it may be that it is only when a child receives their name that it can be said to truly exist as an individual.

That first, personal, name stays with you all your life and marks you out as a full being – legal, social, moral, personal, a formally validated personal label that gives you recognised entry into the full community of humankind. It is your permanent and for the most part ineradicable identifier.

Unlike other labels, it seldom if ever changes from toddler days to school to job to old age. It is the token that singles you out from others at school, work, marriage, retirement, death, your bureaucratic existence in space and time. Birthdays with the recipient's name prominently on the cards and, in some countries, the name-saint's day adds further depth.

---

40 en.wikipedia.org/wiki/Cultural_memory/, en.wikipedia.org/wiki/Collective_memory/, Assmann 2008, Connerton 1989, Genova 2021.

41 Explicated in Mauss 1925 and many anthropological works since.
42 Fuller discussion in Finnegan 2017, 2020.

So too does the repetition of first name(s) for funerals, exorcisms, email messages, and introductions on radio, television, social media, and remote conversations. Names on tombstones and in photographs are often explicitly described as displayed there so that 'the name will not be forgotten'.

If that first name marks an individual's presence in the world and remains with them for life, maybe for eternity, it is in some cases disrupted or forgotten. This is if the name is deliberately changed or removed. A new relationship or a new status is signalled by a new first name – an outwardly small but significant change. At a deeper level, as when someone enters a closed order or secret society, the new name sends a signal to the world, and to the person holding it, that here is a new and different person.

To bring it closer to home – and, eventually, to taxi drivers – during my longitudinal study of names in the context of family history I was startled by the number of repetitions of the *same* first names, drawing me into, and back to, earlier generations: grandparents recalled in grandchildren's names and in the explanation of 'why they had been given that name'. Not just in eastern cultures, often assumed to be more mythically inclined, but here in the down-to-earth west names can carry the symbolic stories of the family; earlier, now dead, forebears can be brought back, in a sense from the cosmic eternal, by their names, re-living in their great-grandchildren. There is a arguably a sense in which, akin to reincarnation, these namesakes are almost the same person.

Take it more widely. Names come in everywhere, more pervasive than they might seem at first sight. Indeed we often seem, perhaps unconsciously, to assume that the *names in themselves* have a kind of inherent power, almost if they are the deepest, enduring, essence of their holder. We are'

constantly coming across, maybe have ourselves uttered passages like

'Hallowed be Thy Name'
'In the name of the lord/ the king/ the law we …'

This background turns out to be surprisingly relevant for taxi drivers' lives. The meanings of their personal names matter. True, the many immigrant taxi drivers in Milton Keynes who come from a foreign-language tradition sometimes use English names for their passengers' convenience. But all know, and among their compatriots regularly use, their true birth-given names.

When asked this name's meaning, many drivers began by saying that they did not know – it is after all quite a personal topic – but then would come out with something like 'I think it may be something like, we'll maybe, 'Kind' ', 'Er, maybe 'Loving God' ', 'The Sun', 'I think it may be some kind of flower', or, shyly, 'I don't know... um, um, something like 'Noble'' or (from an Easy African Asian, 'Lotus', or 'A good man', and were generally pleased that their name was of interest and significance. Despite the apparent hesitation, immigrant drivers were almost always fully conscious of the meanings and value.

Of course they also talked lightheartedly about names or used them to joke. Thus, from a very black Congolese driver, I was greeted with a mock-serious 'The name is Bond, James Bond' or 'I'm Justin Bieber', then a huge grin. Some told me with some amusement about how they they altered their names to make them pronounceable by English speakers – 'Jed' for example or 'Tom' – but then went on 'But my *real* name is … '.

The power of names – often given by grandfathers and thus an emotive link to background and family – can deeply affect life and personality.

Among the taxi drivers I asked there was a wide range of colourful and metaphorical meanings, often seeming to be exactly suited to their bearers' personalities. Examples of these names' meanings were 'Loving God', 'Noble', 'One who is Charitable', 'A Flower', 'Strong and Steadfast', 'Shining', 'A Lion', 'Heaven', 'Humble', 'Radiant', 'Kind', 'A Beautiful Manner of Life', 'One Who Accompanies the Prophet', 'Beloved of God', 'Non-Criminal', 'Strength', 'Wisdom', 'The sun is shining', 'Honoured', 'God's servant', 'Beauty', 'Honest', 'Prince', 'Welcome','"Looking After Others', and so forth, meaningful and often inspiring names.

Drivers from a western background less often knew their names' meanings. So I made a practice of beginning by telling them that the meaning of my own name 'Ruth' was the beautiful – to me – 'Compassion' (now I have come to think of it, I realise that that does indeed go deep in my life, one of the gifts (in several senses) from my parents).

Drivers appreciated this, it seemed – after all telling someone your first name and its meaning is a mark of confidence and outreach, almost (as we have seen) giving them a kind of claim over you. When I asked tentatively about theirs they generally looked thoughtful. A few did indeed know their name's meaning or, for some, its biblical connection. Others were sure their name did not have any meaning but said they might look it up (there are ample sources on the web and in the prolific baby naming books consulted by parents); those who perhaps *did* follow up might have been surprised.

So, names do generally have meanings and this matters, doubtless below as well as above the level of consciousness. This much was scarcely surprising. The striking thing however was how often the name seemed suited to its individual bearer.

When I commented on this to drivers, we often fell into a conversation about whether the bearer was influenced in their life by somehow growing into the name, or whether the name's giver somehow detected that child's inner self in the womb and named it accordingly.

The drivers, thoughtful, were not sure but in the whole they too also felt that it was probably both. The elders who had selected the names, specially the paternal grandfather, important in all traditions, and whom in a way they represented in the present generation, may somehow have seen into who the new child essentially was and the seed, helped by their names, they would become.

And in a way it did seem to be so. You could see the inner character shining through the sometimes tired faces and worn clothes when you learned a driver's name and something of their experiences and what in their lives they had contributed – and, inspired it would seem by the names, continued to strive after.

Among the most articulate about the significance of their names were the many Muslim drivers I met. I did not come across so many drivers from Hindu traditions but for those I did much the same applied. They had – and valued – names with meanings such as 'Freedom', 'Protector', 'Beautiful', 'God in my head'.

I remember especially a Pakistani driver with an IT degree, who, recently redundant from a high level job in a local supermarket, was, in the interim until he found another job he liked, decided on taxi driving; since he already had a car with a satnav this was for him an obvious choice and he was now making a good living that way. It was true that his driving was not essential as his redundancy payment would easily keep him for a year but he preferred to work. Meantime he had put in multiple applications but would only accept a job he thought would be interesting' (he had turned down three as 'not right').

On the face of it, then, he was an engaging and successful go-getter. But he also quietly told me his name. Underlying the surface wordliness was his name. It had the meaning (in English) of 'Green man' – a name, it turns out, that also has significant symbolic import in European and Eastern mythology (elaborated in Anderson 1990). He went on to explain that this was the name both of a prophet and of the saint who was in charge of water and was renowned for having to having brought out water from a sacred fountain in India as something that will live, blessed, for ever. For him this was a significant, inspiring, thread in his life.

Another driver, born in East Africa, had come to the UK after his mother had died in India. His family was now flourishing here, with his son a highly qualified dentist in Cardiff. His Hindu name had the meaning of 'Do a kind thing'. It absolutely fitted his personality.

A driver from Congo named (in English translation) 'Sower of Seed' told me that when he was young he had once heard his mother say he would be a preacher. 'Nonsense', he had thought, 'nothing near my ambitions for my life'. He had come to Britain to study construction management but after a year of that realised it was wrong for him: 'I knew from the Holy Spirit that that was not it'. He went on to take a degree in theology. Though he was now a full-time taxi driver, in his free time he was now a preacher at one of the local Pentecostal churches.

'My sermons are under the control of the Holy Spirit' he explained to me, 'I think about it beforehand but when you speak the Holy Spirit comes into you and utters the words, it is not you. The congregation too is filled with it'. 'So', he ended 'my mother was right and so was the name that my parents, through the Holy Spirit, have given me: Sower of Seed'.

I asked another driver his name and its meaning. He hesitated and then said 'Imagination'. Intrigued I asked if that in any way came out in his life and, if so, in what way. 'Yes, in writing and art'.

That combination turned out to mean hand-written Arabic calligraphy on which he spent many hours of his free time. He showed me one example of his art from the images on his iphone; It was the Muslim declaration of faith, with, at the top, the moon.

This reminded me again of the way that *names* are not just labels but can also in some way play out their bearers' destinies. It comes in western names too, for this is not something limited to taxi drivers, immigrants or non-western traditions. In some cultures the significance of names and naming is more conscious, in others more veiled, perhaps hidden beneath the ordinary course of peoples' lives, but whether explicit or more implicitly, somehow, it seems, affecting them.

Names have implications both for the named themselves, and for those who, knowing the names, interact with them, and for those who inhabit them. This subtle, often disregarded, significance of names is something we need to

add into our accounts of human knowing – for us all, and certainly for MK taxi drivers.

Parallel lives

'Be yourself, no one else will'

Initially to my surprise (I began as ignorant as the next person) I have over time had many deep and unplanned conversations with drivers about such subjects as the reality of dreams as guide to living and/or communication with the dead (something not widely talked about but not limited, sure, to taxi drivers); the beauties and wisdom of language; art; theology (I think of the many sermons – immensely thoughtful sometimes and always deeply felt – that I have received from drivers); nature (many eulogies on the beauties of green Milton Keynes in verdant springs and golden autumns); a soul's testing as it comes to heaven.

Many drivers worked long hours to make ends meet (50-70 hours a week was not uncommon), but even for them taxi driving was a flexible occupation and they valued the way they could always take time off as needed for their family and personal interests. Some drove only part time, leaving plenty of hours, even days, for their other interests: driving as an entry to other, deeper, pursuits.

They explained that these included such things as watching television, sport (specially football and once – to my surprise – the extremely expensive sport of golf), or being a chef, historian, pastor, painter, and much else personal to the individual. Spending time with the family – 'playing with the kids' – figured large, like (with *what* a smile!) 'When I get home, even in the middle of the night, there's my four year old daughter shouting 'Dadee' and rushing up to give me a hug'. Being a musician worked specially well, with driving in the daytime leaving the evenings for performing gigs at pubs or private events.

Most drivers can boast of having at one time or another had someone famous in their cab, Most drivers can boast encountered some celebrated personage.

One London black cab driver from Guyana, for instance, started very silent but fired up when I mentioned having, when a student, heard the charismatic leader Cheddi Jagan speak. Then with great verve he went in to tell a vivid tale of how after his father had come to England he had been working as a manager in night club in London. As in other clubs he was expected to follow the then expected corrupt scheme of paying protection money to the police. His father, on refusing to pay, was arrested and charged. A Welsh QC. Elyleston Morgan defended his father and got him acquitted. 'I'm named Ely for that QC – that makes me partly Welsh, doesn't it'– still excited by the memory – 'That a great man like that would ...'.

Drivers could treasure many precious memories like that, an inspiration behind their workaday lives.

For many drivers, religion, whether Islam, Christianity, Hinduism, Jehovah's Witness or whatever, was a significant strand in their self identities, including for those who did not attend formal religious services. As one said, in a general sentiment typical of many, ' from a Hindu background but I do not go the local temple. It is *goodness* that matters not the temple'.

From a Muslim I heard a long and heart-felt disquisition on the importance of honesty in life, and then on human destiny. 'God lays down our destiny for us at birth, then it is up to us to choose the right one, the one that leads to happiness, or the wrong one that may seem happy for a while but not in the end, 'God gives everyone two angels, one on the right who records good deeds, one on left who records the bad'.

Where had he learned this I queried.

'Some from my religion [Islam], some from sitting at the feet of wise people and learning from them'.

Many, too, are the uplifting 30-minute long sermon equivalents I have heard expounding truths related such texts as ' God is great, whatever his name …', 'Only believe in God, you will be saved', 'I was called in a dream to be a pastor and when I speak the Spirit of the Lord speaks through my lips …', 'The Quran/ Bible/ sacred writings are my hope and my trust … '.

Another day I was driven by Mohamed from Bangladesh. For him what gave his life meaning was his study of religious texts, above all the Quran. He explained the calligraphic device hanging inside his windscreen and thus constantly in his sight as 'It is the name of Allah'.

The Arabic words on the other side were a beautiful prayer relating to transport, translated something like 'In the name of Allah. Praise be to Allah. Glory unto Him Who created this transportation for us, though we were unable to create it on our own. And unto our Lord we shall return'.

He followed this up by emphasising vehemently that there is no single way in religion: 'It can be Christianity, it can be Islam, God is the same for all of us, each must find

his own way and then God will tell him if it is right. He must keep trying'.

'How do you do that?' I asked.

'*Study*. Studying the Quran whenever free. Everything, everything, is there'.

Others do not use explicitly religious terminology but still go behind everyday practicalities to invoke moral concepts. 'You can say 'God' or 'Allah' as you like, but for me, every day, it is 'Being a Good Man' '.

The drivers, it seemed, tried to keep their work personas separate from what they regarded as their parallel life outside the taxi industry, whether this was artist, parent, writer, religious minister or whatever.

All these aspects, varying of course with the individual, formed important dimensions of drivers' 'real' (or, if you like, 'dream') parallel lives outside their taxi being. For behind all was not 'the taxi driver' but the deeper, persisting, 'me'.

One who seemed well aware of this aspect was Kojo from Ghana. He had studied planning as one of his three subjects while doing a Leeds Business School degree and found it had opened his eyes to what was around him.

'Milton Keynes has been so well planned', he said, 'Why would you want to live somewhere else when you can get all this here. My kids can go to a park within walking distance and we have a great built environment all round: a combination of trees and nature with social areas and new building'.

He explained that he had got interested in the city's planning as he drove round. With his background he was looking at things other people might not even see or would pass without noticing.

'Look at the daffodils', he continued, pointing out of the window, 'and the buds on the spring trees. And the way they change in the autumn'.

For him life was clearly not just roads, driving, routes, but the magic of nature that he encountered as he passed. 'One day', he added 'I will go back to Ghana and live in a beautiful old house there and help in the planning. I will be myself'.

On another occasion I asked Ahmed from Bangladesh, a long-time taxi driver planning to qualify as an electrician, what he would say at the gate of heaven that *he,* essentially, was. I expected him, naturally, to say driver or electrician or Bangladeshi, or, possibly family man. 'A chef'. It turned out that fine cooking, something he had first come across in Scotland just after he had arrived in Britain, was his truest love. He didn't think, he added with a smile, that there would be openings for him for a full time job on this earth.

'What about heaven?' I asked, 'will you cook there?' 'In heaven there is no cooking', he replied seriously and unhesitatingly, 'but all that we want will be there, by God's wish'. So – behind the taxi driver, a God-fearing would-be chef (I couldn't help thinking that he surely *would* be cooking in heaven).

For another the answer to my same question was 'A reader'. 'What do you read?' I asked. 'Oh – ah, anything. Well, since you ask, psychology and philosophy'. 'Like – ?' 'Um, Freud. And German philosophers'.

Bella from Bulgaria put it more simply, in words that many might resonate with: 'That happy. Happy that I love my daughter. Happy that I love my grandchildren, and nature, and my rescued cat named Reah, and that it is *good* to be happy'.

Abdul from Bangladesh responded on similar lines: 'To be a good man it doesn't matter if you are Muslim, doesn't matter if you are Christian, you must be a good man. And unless you are a good man you will not enter heaven'.

I omitted to put the same question to Surah, from India. But I know well what he would have said. 'An artist'. He showed me some of his pictures, stored in his phone, but, modest, would not let me have copies, The colours and the designs were stunning. 'They illustrate the last great battle in the Ramayana, the famous one', he says, 'they're inspired by the great tradition of Hindu art'. I looked that up later – his simple yet intricate art was indeed part of that tradition.

Another – a Yoruba from Nigeria, an experienced driver and trained carer – after a pause for thought answered the same question differently. 'Two things. First of all I would give thanks for my life, the world, my years here, I would express my appreciation for all that'. Another pause. I don't know … It is a good question – I have still many years to live, to find the answer, to find myself'.

'Where am I myself, the whole man, the true man? Where am I with the mark of God upon my brow?' (Ibsen)

Here are some other people that I came across driving taxis and that at first astonished me (though given the diversity of drivers – of *people* – I should not have been surprised). I was told such things, remember, in the liminal close space of a taxi cab where people find it safe to open up on things that they are otherwise quiet, even secretive, about, and where, as in dream, they have, somehow, an obligation to tell the truth. It was always a privilege to hear of these other sides to their lives.

The reader and thinker

Faisan from Pakistan talked about the relation between Urdu and Hindi, something I had not previously understood. In speech they are mutually intelligible, he explained, apart from a scattering of a few different words, and both have widely read written forms.
Hindi is perhaps the most popular, but written

Urdu, linked to Persia, with which he was clearly well acquainted, is more literary and poetic.

His favourite writer (unprompted – we had just been discussing books and writing in a general way) was Jalāl al-Dīn Muḥammad Rūmī, popularly known as Rumi, the mediaeval mystic poet of the Islamic Golden Age in Persia, conveyer of deep Sufic, but at the same time universal, mystic wisdom. He added that we should also consider Hafez, another Persian lyric poet a little later whose works also expressed divine inspiration and whom I had not at that point heard of – he kindly wrote down his name for me. He loved Rumi above all, whom of course, unlike me, he had read in the original: 'he is so deep, his stories too, that wisdom goes right inside you'.

We went on to talk about different religions.

'Which is the largest religion in the world?' he asked me, then answered himself 'Humanity. That is where we must begin'.

And then 'What are the three most important things?', answered by

The sun – it shines equally on all, whatever religion they call themselves.

The river – we can all drink from it, whatever religion we call ourselves.

The earth – we can all tread on it whatever religion we call ourselves'.

He would have continued, but we had arrived.

The Human Relations enthusiast

The taxi driver Bashir ('Good news' – I try to live that) who had been born in northern Ghana whisked me swiftly and efficiently to my destination with the typically Ghanaian broad warm smile – I thought , again, that it is the best smile in the world. He had come to

Britain to get a professional qualification that would be internationally recognised, and was now part way through a course in human relations at a highly regarded local university. He had chosen that subject because of his experience of being in a job in Ghana where he had seen the workers being really badly treated: 'I wanted to be a position to put that kind of thing right'.

Being a student in Britain had been expensive but he had been able to pay the first instalment of his fees (without which he would not have got a visa) and buy a car, now his taxi, from money he had earned from working in communications in Ghana after he had left school. Now, during the university summer vacation 'I can work full time as a taxi driver, the rest of the year part-time to pay for my course'.

He seemed to be greatly enjoying his course and was prepared to talk about it endlessly. Noticing my ignorance he explained: 'HR – Human relations – is all about the happiness of workers. What happens when something has gone wrong? *You* are the one responsible. What happens when workers want to negotiate a better wage? *You* are the one responsible. What happens when someone is dismissed? *You* are the one responsible, *you* sort the problems'.

Once qualified his plan was to go back to Ghana and take any human relations job he could get. It was clear that he did not think of himself as a taxi driver – that was only a temporary means to an end – but as an HR person totally committed to the contribution that, once qualified, he would be able to make to human ('*human*') relations in his home country, his whole reason for coming here and, for now, temporarily, driving a taxi.

For me, meeting him and hearing his enthusiasm was an education in itself.

The musician[43]

We were on the way to the airport, not talking much, in a quiet expensive electric car driven by an attractive 40-ish man in smart uniform and tie. We stopped at a road junction and I heard that the radio was on, very quiet – to my surprise and pleasure it was a Beethoven piano sonata.

We talked about music. It turned out that this was Steve's central interest, he listened to classical music 7-9 hours a day. He was a performer on guitar, piano, keyboard, also once a singer, and had in the past been a player in some well-known local bands. He also spent a lot of his time 'composing – that is, playing around and improvising on my guitar to please myself'.

As a composer – he spoke of this as 'a gift' – musical inspiration comes to him, he said, at odd unexpected times. It can be when he's waiting around in his taxi for a passenger so he always keeps an audio recorder there for these moments.

'How did you get into taxis?' I asked.

'Oh, taxis? About that? My driving days started off as a courier delivering parcels, then I joined a transport firm and worked my way up to being a manager in transport logistics. I was a transport manager for about 5 years but the company got taken over and the office closed. So I was out of work for 6 months and ended up going into taxis'.

Building on his transport manager experience, he was now running one of the best home-to-airport taxi services in the area, effortlessly (it seemed) organising a number of drivers.

'It is still about transport. But music, performing in a band, is what it's really about'.

He explained how he'd got started in music – 'just a few chords on the bass guitar – toddler stage you could say – but I found I had a good feel for rhythm and after a while I formed a band with my younger brother and school friends that we used to jam together with. For three years we were out and about with the band almost every night'.

He and his band had indeed had some success, the highlight being playing for the charity 'Children in Need', in Johnny Dankworth's famous 'Stables' venue on the edge of Milton Keynes, photographed on the front page of a local paper.

Steve reflected on their early days. 'I remember our first rehearsal so well, in a garage in Stony Stratford. Then our first ever gig in the main arena in Wolverton, years ago – I think it's now been turned into some sort of church. I remember being really proud of my brother, a guitarist. He'd begun by just jamming with various people, then when he was 16 he started getting lessons – amazing, within a couple of years he was really good, it was incredible really'.

Alas, his brother had committed suicide, Steve still didn't know why. He said he himself had been in denial over this for months, but the conviction that he *had* to carry on, for his brother, saved him. And above all *music*.

---

[43] This is based on conversations during two long taxi rides and also (unlike other accounts) on a subsequent meeting over lunch where he allowed me to record some of his story, of which certain extracts are, with his permission, repeated here.

Also his marriage and children – but that was hard too: his first son died after 10 days, and was now buried with butterflies on his tomb (for a while we discussed butterflies and soul and all that: 'A butterfly's life is short – but long enough' – a lovely saying).

To get on as a group and – in a way the same thing – a composer, he pointed out, you needed an agent or manager, but like so many he had had difficulty in achieving that. On our second trip together, however, he told me he'd had success.

'I've got an agent! *and* an established female artist. But there are some legal issues tied up with her commitment to another label, so though she would like it she might not be able to sign up with us, it's quite a closed shop'. Taxi driver or not, getting on in the music business is clearly no easy matter.

He went on, reflectively, 'The musician in me is like a parallel world really, it's the end in sight. During my everyday life in the normal world, I step in and out of it. How I feel when I play is – well for minutes you're a different person. You feel like you're in a protective bubble of performance, a parallel life – I suppose a footballer feels like that during a match, moving into another world. When you know it's going really well, when you feel like you are in a world that nobody can penetrate until I finish – well it's amazing.

'And for the songs I compose – I find the best ones are just sitting there, already there in my mind … I always keep my acoustic guitar in my bedroom, and I can't walk past it without picking it up. Then it depends what happens. I might find myself playing a cover version of a song I already know, or I might sit there and start playing cold and all of a sudden you've got an idea that just popped into your head and that's wonderful! The melody just comes from nowhere. And then you find you have the words too, maybe about experiences and feelings of loss, remembering my brother, or it can morph into something different from its origins. I keep a dictaphone – look – in my taxi

too, for any ideas that come as I'm waiting around – there's a lot of that if you're a taxi driver.

'Some of my best stuff was written during my darkest times, perhaps that's when the musician in you comes to the forefront. The real me'. Now he plans to write his life – *not* about his life as a successful taxi-driver and hard-working owner of a successful taxi firm as I'd assumed, just 'life – music; my brother; my wife and family'.

He helped me out with my luggage, then drove off with a pleasant wave – taxi driver, helper, musician.

The farmer

Once you show an interest, drivers often talk fondly of their home country. Many of them have parents who are still farmers there (livestock farmers in Bangladesh or Pakistan for instance), some of them in businesses and/or well off. When they go home for a visit, as they try to do once a year or when they have earned enough for the fare, they often take it for granted that they will help out as usual on the farm. They are happy to do so and, if encouraged, to talk about it when they return to this country.

One, from the Ivory Coast in West Africa, was clearly still deeply a farmer at heart – and as far as he could in practice too. His second name meant 'sun' – 'just right for a farmer' he said with a pleased smile. He was at first shy of talking about his farming, assuming that I would not be sympathetic, but it soon came pouring out.

Farming had long been the livelihood and roots and life of his family. He spoke of it with a degree of homesickness, less perhaps for his country than for the deep love of tending his land which for the moment he could not do. It was moving to hear him speak of it, and clearly, as well as practical and down to earth, it was intensely heartfelt revelation of his genuine, deep, grounded, self.

83

'At first I wasn't sure what I wanted to do, but I saw television programme about growing food for children in Ethiopia' – I could tell from his body language that he felt very strongly about the famines in Ethiopia and Somalia – 'I decided I wanted to be farmer myself and feed children. I came here to learn European agriculture methods'.

When he came to Britain he had managed to get work ('unskilled') on a farm here, then, on the back of that, was accepted a one year further education study in Milton Keynes. Next he embarked on a 3 year agriculture degree at the University of Essex ('great course, wonderful teachers') where he was now in his final year.

'It's a great arrangement, with real practical work on the farms the university owns. Instead of the usual student fee you pay £9000 a year to rent a plot (I depend on my driving for the money). It's wonderful, I can practise with *every* kind of crop and animal – cattle, sheep, pigs, chickens (my favourite – dual purpose: eggs *and* meat), goats, even llamas. I'm driving at the moment because it's university vacation and I'm not needed just now in farm.

'And you know what? For the first time ever in the course, I managed to not only farm it well but actually to get it to return a *profit!*'

He explained that behind all this he owned a patch of inherited land in the Ivory Coast, his home. His brother was currently keeping it in cultivated heart on his behalf and sending him regular reports. When he's finished the course he plans to return to farm in Ivory Coast.

'It's family land. It used to be thick forest, full of bad bad spirits. When I was boy I was forbidden to go there (and I didn't because once in there you would never be found again)' By now most of the forest had been cut down and they were growing cassava, the staple crop, and some rice. 'I am in touch with

UNICEF, the arrangement is that I provide the land and labour, they provide tractors, equipment, seed and all that. I grow the food, and it will all be for UNICEF, for *children*'.

He lit up at the idea, clearly deeply committed. 'I'll also teach local people about recent farming ideas, so we can have a perfect combination of local traditional farming practice – it has its good sense too – and modern European knowledge'. So, at last, he could be his true self.

I rather think that of all the wonderful drivers I met, *his* combination of ancient and modern knowledge was the most inspiring of them all (maybe deep down I too, (like everyone?) have, somewhere, a farming heritage?).

John Shabaya, in turn failed Kenyan schoolboy, garden worker, church assistant, Cambridge graduate, minister, school teacher, and taxi driver.

The theologian from Kenya

A quiet elderly man drove me to where I was staying and as I fumbled around for my money he asked me politely what I was doing here in Cambridge. I explained that I had an appointment the next day with Dr Rowan Williams, explaining kindly, as I assumed would be needed, that he had been the previous Archbishop of Canterbury. He smiled and said 'He was my tutor'.

It turned out that this taxi driver, brought up in a hut in East Africa, had studied theology in the University of Cambridge, then after graduating and further study had been ordained and spent a career as a religious studies teacher. Now retired he was driving a taxi to raise funds for the school he had founded in Kenya. Whew – not what I 'd expected. Not long after, he expanded his story into an engrossing memoir published in 2020[44], previewing and reflecting back on his life in the hope it would be an inspiration and encouragement to others.

John is now writing further books and also, no doubt, still comes across as a quiet, inconspicuous, taxi driver.

It opens in near-poetic terms

'Here I am
From rags to fine garbs.
From a mud hut to Cambridge.
From shacks to Cambridge
From Humble Beginnings
To an Incredible Journey.
This is the story of my life.

Hear the voice of a village boy.
Born of very deprived, poor parents.
Born of illiterate parents,
But I dreamed big dreams.
Hear my voice.
I loved, Wanted,
And longed to travel the world.
I failed my Primary School Exams,
Meant to catapult learners
to a great and bright future.
Meant to launch me,
into a pre-eminent and brilliant future.
Therefore Doomed!

I Constantly heard voices of failure.
The community around me,
My Primary School teachers,
kept telling me:
'You are a failure!
Do not dream young man!
Dreams don't always come true.'

They reiterated,
'Just like your father,
You will never make it!
You have failed to get your KEY
The key to life,

The opener of the future for learners
The opener of your dreams.

Your dreams are over.
Do not dream again!
Do not dream any-more!
You have no hope.
Your future is doomed.'
But I never, never, ever gave up.
I continued to dream,
To dream against all odds.
Here I am
A Cambridge University graduate, UK.
A High School teacher, UK.
Head of a Department,
A Subject Leader, UK.

Taught for over 19 years in UK.
I have been a clergy,
I have been an Officer,
Kenya Defence Forces,
Up to the rank of Major.
Travelled extensively,
All over the world.
Retired from teaching, UK,
But not tired.

Never really stopped
Working and volunteering.
I am a Charity Worker.
Founder Room2Excel
An Educational Charity.
Founder & Director:
Atsinafa Education Centre,

Western Kenya,
A legacy to my illiterate mother.
A Translator and Proof-reader.
A Cab, a Taxi Driver.
I endeavour to give back,
To the community.

Read and hear the voice of
Hope and determination.
Hear the voice of encouragement.
Read my dare to dream,
And dare to try story.

Read and hear:
How one can emerge:
From subsequent ashes,
From dust,
From failure to success.
From a remote village,
In Kenya to Cambridge, UK
From an illiterate home,
From a mud hut,
To Cambridge University.
How one can get the money,
To study at Cambridge University.

I am the boy,
born in Ishanji Village,
Born in Western Kenya
Grew up in a mud hut.
And ended up in Cambridge
Yes, I am'.

This *incredible journey* is the story of my life!

[44] Published as a full autobiographical account in Rev. John Shabaya,
From mud hut to Cambridge: an incredible journey, Balestier Press, 2020.

The piano restorer

'I was in a pub', the driver said, 'and someone was playing a piano. It was inspiring. Amazing. It turned my life round'.

It led him to buy a cheap, old, piano for himself. But a piano tuner he got in touch with told him it wasn't up to much. That fired his interest and he signed up as an apprentice with the local piano-makers, Bletchley Pianos in Fenny Stratford at one end of Bletchley.

By now he was now fully qualified ('but still learning every day – those amazing pianos …') and immediately recognised the make and background of my and my daughter's pianos from my vague description. He was a regular keyboard player with a well-known local jazz band ('the longest lasting one in the area' – I knew it well), as well as working part-time in the piano section of a local music shop, and, greatest satisfaction of all, running his own piano restorer shop in nearby Newport Pagnell, where he lived, specialising in buying up old pianos (Yamaha his favourite) and fixing them. He was making about the same amount of money from that and from his taxi driving – but it was clear which of the two came from the heart.

The dream-catching SAS Captain

The driver reached across to open the door for me and gave a brief smile as I got in, waiting to see whether or not I wanted to talk. I wasn't sure but I could feel he was full of vibrant energy, sitting there looking lean, and sinewy, and mentally tough. And yes, as I looked again, immensely strong and at the same time totally relaxed.

We set off, he handled the car easily, somehow scarcely noticing but with full control.

As usual we began with his name – Cam. I wasn't at all sure that was really it but it

didn't really matter. I asked further. What came across forcefully – shocking me – was his next statement: 'If you really want to know, the youngest Captain ever to qualify for the SAS'. Even I knew that was quite some claim. The SAS (The United Kingdom Special Air Service) is known to be a highly select force who operate on the most difficult and dangerous assignments of all, like hostage rescue or lightning snatch assignments, with all the mental and physical toughness needed to evade or, if necessary, survive capture.

He talked about how for him, as for many, it had started in childhood. He had always been interested in mechanical things and making things work as well as challenging himself against hard obstacles. In his teens he decided that the army was for him. So he learnt about flying aeroplanes, which he had found no problem at all. I asked if he had considered aiming for the Red Arrows formation flyers, but apparently he had thought trying for the SAS looked more challenging: after all, like them, he always spent many hours of the day making himself the fittest of anyone around. So why not try?

He liked the sound of the incredibly demanding entry requirements and the over-90% failure rate. So with 200 others he began on the gruelling 7 month selection process.

Cam went in to explain that first he had to complete basic army training tests, followed by demonstrating expert knowledge about aeroplanes, something he found it easy. Then came hugely challenging personal fitness conditions – among them, he said, being able to complete 50 sit-ups in two minutes, a 1.5-mile run in 10 and a half minutes and march of 8 miles carrying 25 lbs of equipment in two hours. Later it was running 4 miles in 30 minutes and swimming 2 miles in 90 minutes.

But the really fearsome ordeal, he went on, was the excruciating 20 hour endurance test.

Everyone dreaded this. It was climbing up and down the near-3000 foot high Pen y Fan mountain in the Brecon Beacons carrying full equipment, a horrific experience in which candidates could – and did – indeed die. He didn't go into details but admitted that even he found it near lethal. He continued by describing how after he was qualified and experienced, one of his duties had been to follow up from the rear with support for those attempting the test. He commented that those who drank all their water at the start or started off too fast could not carry on. 'I found them lying on the ground, near death. You turn them on their front and inject them in the bottom – not dignified but the only way to save their lives'.

He touched lightly but didn't expand on what came later: something about being thrown out of an aeroplane to survive for a month on roots or whatever they could find, the gruelling interrogation-survival skills bit, then the two – two out the 200 starters – who had got through being assigned to duty in Syria.

Just now, he told me, he was between assignments and found taxi driving a good distraction while he waited for his next call, due in a few months time.

There was clearly more but we had arrived at our destination and he drove smoothly off to his next fare. I was left hoping to meet him again, but I never did. Whew!

I had been carried along with his story at the time. Afterwards I felt sceptical. Surely this was a case of the wishful thinking common among young men or a make-believe story to while away the long waiting-around life of a taxi driver. Anyhow if truly a member of the secretive SAS would he, could he, ever have divulged this to an outsider?

The detail seemed in his favour, borne out when I looked up on the web to see how SAS people were tested and trained – it all fitted.

But then of course, vivid as were all the small details he recounted, he too could have tracked them down. It cut both ways.

Somewhat in his favour was his physique. I don't think I've ever before met someone so clearly fit – wiry and sinewy rather than bulkily strong – and with a kind of controlled inner vibrancy. He also gave a somehow relaxed impression of command: someone you would automatically look to for leadership in confusion or danger.

Would someone of his obvious quality be content just to be a local taxi driver? But then again, SAS Reservists, *active* individuals above all, aren't just going to be sitting twiddling their thumbs while waiting for their next assignment. They must after all live and carry on their lives and be found *somewhere*.

So why *not* as a taxi driver? The flexible demands of taxi driving would enable him to continue with his keep-fit exercise and strengthening projects and further education.

And if taxi driving, why not in in the pleasant surroundings of Milton Keynes? And why, with my frequent use of taxis, might I not meet him?

 still uncertain. Perhaps I believe him. But in any case perhaps on one – not every – level it doesn't matter. We live in a dream as well as an everyday world. And whether or not literal truth, I could see that he – the dreamcatcher SAS Reservist – was truly caught into his experience, himself, his crafted real dream into which he had allowed me to enter in the confidentiality of taxi liminal space.

What I saw in my encounter with Cam, is that taxi drivers too capture dreams and that for all of us, drivers or not, dream can feel as close, as important, as 'reality', and 'real' experience as dreamlike and somehow entranced within oneself as any other life experience.

It is something not to be forgotten in our understanding of human culture.

The devoted family man and deep-down poet

At first he was quiet and seemed disinclined to talk. But when I asked about his name he became animated, in completely fluent English. He is 'Sunni', meaning, he said, 'light' or 'energy' (suited him). That was the quick name he used to English speakers, he also had a longer more complex one in his native Urdu.

Sunni was born in Pakistan and came here after school and his first job, to join his Pakistani wife who was settled here. She was at that time a care worker with old people though she had now moved, he said, into part-time voluntary care work. Like so many he himself ultimately came from farming stock. His grandparents were farmers, but his father had done well, been educated, moved to the city and worked in the computer industry, by now well off.

When he himself came to England he had had a variety of jobs, starting with being a porter in Oxford colleges (including my own college of Somerville – no wonder his English was good!) – a highly responsible guard rather than just carrier job – then a porter in Asda supermarkets (at the time good employers, he said). But then he had a back problem so decided to become a taxi driver where you could sit and be supported by a backrest.

He owned his car, bought with a loan from his family – the wider family, that is, including his in–laws – now, a matter of pride, fully repaid. He was paying £75 a week to his taxi firm, Starline, for what he termed their 'communications box' – other firms charged more, he said, though it varied a bit according to the time of day or night, and was making enough every week to get by. He preferred just to work in the day and with fairly short hours so that he could be with his family.

He was clearly extremely proud of his children, specially his twin daughters of 11 at a local primary school, one very good at painting, the other at computers. He said he did not yet know what they would want to do eventually but didn't deny it when I surmised it might be something professional: 'something good'.

They all go back from time to time to Pakistan, he said, the previous year being the most recent time. 'The children don't *speak* Urdu but they can understand it. It's good for them to meet their cousins. By now half the family is in Pakistan, half in this country, we belong to both. both, and I love Urdu'.

He was now, like many immigrant taxi drivers, proud to be a British citizen for which he qualified to apply after three years residence – a condition he approved of. He had a great feeling for refugees and immigrants, just then especially for the Syrian refugees; 'I do what I can to help as an individual with money and goods. Islam is a religion of charity'.

He liked music –'old style' he said – and would have loved to be able to sing but ''I don't know how' (it sounded to me as if he would have a lovely deep bass voice if he tried). He said that he had written a bit about his life: 'some time ago, just jottings about everyday happenings and people I've met'. When I asked, he said he had no thoughts of publishing his writing. He was too modest to let me see any.

He had also written poetry, composed in various places, presumably in the beautiful sonic language of Urdu but perhaps in English too. I said it could be of great interest but again he declined to show or speak any of it.

We had arrived and he dropped me off, courteous as ever, at my door and drove off, just another anonymous taxi driver, to most people, no doubt, seemingly of no interest, no personal story of his own to tell.

THERE

Chapter 10: Just a taxi driver

It is hard to know how I can best sum up findings of such complexity and unique humanity. Let me attempt it however, even if it risks leading into elusive, even somewhat numinous territory.

During these fuse years I have many many individuals, many lives, many unique, rich, fonts of understanding. Here were human beings, humans who – here, now, as for centuries – can be seen as the ultimate treasures of our planet.

Overall they were impressive.

It is true that during my taxi rides I naturally encountered the courteous helpful side of a driver's nature and behaviour. This is after all part of our expectations of what a taxi driver should be like, the implicit contract that he is trained for, that we enter on when we get into a taxi. Outside of that, for I all I know, he (or she) might behave in some horrible antisocial way. I can only tell of my experience as I observed it. That was almost all good.

So I ended up, and I hope have conveyed, with a very positive impression of taxi drivers. Do not mistake me. Taxi drivers are human like the rest of us. They can no doubt be obtuse as well as reflective; bad as well as virtuous; selfish, inhumane and arrogant as well as kind: I have met some of each though immensely more of the good than the bad. So I do not want to end by either demonising or (if it is a word) angellisising them – they are all people with their own individual characteristics.

But there are also some general things I would like to point out in conclusion, the corollary of their situation as both drivers of the roads and, for the most part, migrants from cultures afar. First, their incomer status can remind us of how much we have learnt, and still have to learn, from the wisdoms of other climes and traditions. Of these, taxi drivers, with their varied immigrant backgrounds are, perhaps unawares, true repositories and in a position, daily, to share them with us. A perspective from a different background helps us to scrutinise taken-for-granted assumptions (if, that is, we are prepared to listen – as taxi drivers, up to a point at least, do and must).

And then, as a category taxi drivers have certain characteristics not widely shared. Like priests and therapists they are in a special position of hearing confidences, but their calling, unlike theirs, is not to comfort or forgive or heal but just in a short time-limited separate space to hear. Whether or not they recall what they hear, it is a valuable role. As a condition of their profession they regularly inhabit that liminal, shared, space and time, where, however briefly and perhaps not fully consciously, they can gather wisdom from patient waiting and half-focused driving, and from the deep if hidden truth of names and destiny. Inevitably they hear and learn from the diverse human beings – good and bad, new and old, local and foreign – with whom they interact. In ways that they are probably not themselves consciously aware of, they can regarded as holders and sharers of knowledge for our time.

Finally let us never forget that every human in these times – indeed in any time – is unique and different. But taxi drivers seem, through the circumstances of their work, to have a special potential for the purveying and sharing of wisdom. More than just the some-time knights of the roads – itself a precious role – taxi drivers are also, it might be argued, in some ways the philosophers of our times.

They are there, but so often not really seen as fully there. Each is just – a taxi driver, a human.

THE END

Appendix 1: Sources and methods

As for all anthropologists, and to an extent, and where feasible, researchers in other disciplines too, the key source and method of this account is *participant observation*. This took place over a period of five years in Milton Keynes, boosted further by over 50 years residence in the area, and, to a lesser extent, research elsewhere.

To be clear, participant observation is what it says: participating – immersed – in a culture and at the same time observant, objectively and analytically, of what is going on around you, and (following a more recent development), also actively and sensitively aware of your own part in it.

I also relied greatly on a second and long tried method in both anthropology and several other disciplines – *interviews:* in this case informal interviews, mostly of about 20-30 minutes, more like conversations really, with several hundred taxi drivers. Whenever feasible (not possible in black cabs or during the 2020-21 covid restrictions) I sat in the front seat, thus next to the driver, close. There, we tended naturally to exchange mini life stories – family origins, children, jobs, background, aspirations – something most people are prepared to do in relaxed and mutually friendly settings.

At first I did not think of these friendly interactions as 'interviews'. But from a methodology viewpoint that is in fact what they were: interviews in the (recognised) category of *semi-structured interviews* – semi-structured in the sense of not consisting of preset and unvarying questions or written questionnaires or for yes/no responses, but partly 'structured' in the sense that I tended to raise roughly the same topics frequently.

The immigrant drivers (by far the majority) were regularly outgoing and articulate – again and again I met with smiles, not least those warmest ones from Ghanians. Even the (very) few of English origin were mostly friendly and prepared to talk. Luckily for me this after all is the expected demeanour and courtesy expected, indeed required, of taxi drivers.

I did not make notes during the journeys but tried to write down what I remembered of what I felt were the points of interest as soon as I could afterwards. I have a reasonably good memory for words and those that I have put in quote marks in this account are based on that (I did occasionally, with their permission, audio-record drivers' comments during the journey to aid and check my memory but I did not in practice find this rather fiddly method particularly useful and did not use it much at all).

Besides participant observation and informal interviews with taxi drivers in Milton Keynes I also spent some time in taxi journeys and conversation in London, Cambridge, Birmingham, Belfast and some other British cities, also briefly in cities in Europe and America, and more extensively during several visits to New Zealand.

Among drivers in these other cities there were of course unique contexts and personalities, but overall I was impressed to find similar patterns elsewhere to those described in this account for Milton Keynes - immigration (if from a range of differing backgrounds), relations between drivers and operating taxi firms, trends in driver characteristics, taxi drivers' overarching roles and qualifications, and above all their human qualities *outside* of their taxi-industry selves. This comparative experience enhanced my understanding of Milton Keynes taxi drivers and increased my confidence in the account given here.

On other sources, I went beyond what have been traditional anthropological methods (though in fact now increasingly used by anthropologists): *documentary and secondhand*

---

[45] Apart from some visits abroad, I have lived in Milton Keynes since 1969 and have also researched there for two previous books (Finnegan 1989/2007 and 1998/2019) which complement this one, together with a short preliminary preview of these findings (Finnegan 2021).

sources. There are a number of vivid firsthand accounts by taxi drivers (listed in the Select References) which are from time to time quoted here, extending my understanding of taxi drivers' varied personal experiences and reflections, and of some of the things that they heard or passed on. In addition I was helped by certain archive sources (especially the Mass Observation Archive), newspaper reports, and articles on the internet, both personal and general: for example on the taxi companies, national statistics and local council requirements (the most important are noted in the Select References). Such sources were sometimes extremely informative, as were adverts and images.

For the historical sections on the history of hired transport and of Milton Keynes I drew on the usual library and internet sources, noted where relevant in the References.'

Every research setting has its own characteristics so let me say a bit more about this one. I explained in the preface how, at first unintentionally, I came to be involved in the world(s) of taxi drivers, and then decided to note and, eventually, write up my observations. This was not the kind of full-time immersion, far from one's own culture, once thought typical of anthropology but rather something that – characteristic of the driver-passenger interaction – took place on occasion as needed and just from time to time between other commitments.'

Anthropological fieldwork often relies on a relatively limited number of trusted and frequent informants (nowadays, better, usually termed 'consultants') who, often themselves becoming interested in the research questions, provide key information on a regular basis to deepen the scattered information gathered in other ways.

This method was not feasible in this research, where given the participant observation focus,

contacts necessarily consisted of the fleeting interactions characteristic of driver-passenger meetings. Given that there were and are hundreds of taxi drivers in Milton Keynes it was not to be expected that I would often if ever meet the same driver again, and in fact I very seldom did. I sometimes tried to create a longer-term link by following up by email or phone but without response so I soon gave up on that.

The one exception was two longer rides to the airport with the musician Steve, topped by a more lengthy discussion that we set up over lunch (summarised in Chapter 9) but that was the end of it. Otherwise rather than the method of using regular informants/ consultants this account has instead relied on putting together a series of vignettes of separate individuals occasions, supplemented by the other sources mentioned above.

Social scientists and oral historians are nowadays rightly concerned about the ethical dimensions of how they conducted their research so let me say something about that too.

There has been a welcome change in the last couple of generations away from terms like 'informants', 'subjects', or 'data', to 'consultants' or 'colleagues', and to emphasising the idea of cooperation rather than top-down researcher as against researched. There is also, now, an idea that it is only fair, indeed obligatory, in most research settings to be open about the fact that research *is* being undertaken.

Confidentiality in order not to harm people by revealing their identities has been one key principle in this change. At one point this resulted in an almost total ban on divulging individual names at all. Nowadays it is recognised that this needs to be a matter of context and the relevant individuals' preferences. Some individuals, as in my earlier

---

[46]   See further in Anon 2022, Bochner 2016, Davies 2008.
[47]   One reason for the protracted (five years) timescale of this project.

account of Milton Keynes amateur musicians (1989), positively *wanted* their names to be known and their doings publicised, while among those telling their life stories in a later account (Finnegan 1998) some preferred their true names to be revealed, others did not. It is up to the researcher to observe these wishes.

In this study, a few taxi drivers said they preferred not to have their names used, but most did not seem to care much one way or another. To be on the safe side I have in almost every case (apart from a couple who wanted their real names known) used fictitious names for individuals and gone easy on attaching specific information to individuals that might reveal identity. On the other hand the personal details are all authentic as are all the places mentioned.

The photographs of individuals and other images of a personal nature, including their vehicles, are genuine and were taken with the subject's permission.

On a more general note I regularly (though not invariably if I was merely checking general rather than personal information) made a practice of telling the drivers that I was writing a book about taxi drivers' lives. After a moment of somewhat startled surprise and then pleasure, once into their own accounts they tended to forget that or were more interested in asking about my other writing.

Once sure of my open-minded interest, they mostly seemed – like anyone – to enjoy talking about themselves and telling their own stories (it was sometimes quite hard to get away when we had arrived). More than one said they had often thought about writing an account of their life but had not yet got round to it. A few were more taciturn, but the only real exception was an English driver well known by other as morose and bad-tempered

(one commented, with sympathy, 'he has been having family problems').

Since taxi drivers are aware that they tend to have an undeservedly bad, or anyway, demeaning reputation they tended to be glad to have a possible chance to set the record straight, But, as I say, I undertook not, unless they wished this, to give their true names.

In light of the fleeting nature of the interactions with individual drivers this account could not rely on the intensively studied in-depth case studies of many anthropological and similar accounts, Nevertheless I did not wish to remain just with sketching general patterns, necessary as that often was to set the record straight. Indeed resting content with that would have run counter to my increasing awareness of each driver's unique individuality. So as this account proceeds it tends to move away from generalities into giving increasing attention to specific examples which in turn led me into the elusive and, as it were, spiritual dimensions of human lives.

At any rate, I hope that as a result I have given sufficient clues to the idea that lumping them together into the easy-seeming generic category of 'taxi drivers' or 'just a taxi driver' is in reality a whole variegated series of unique, deeply individual, thinking and feeling human beings.

Appendix 2: Some further taxi drivers' quotes and sayings

This extends the sayings in Chapter 8 heard on my drives or collected in other sources about, or to, or by, taxi drivers.

The idea of Twitter started with me working in dispatch since I was 15 years old, where taxi cabs or firetrucks would broadcast where they were and what they were doing (Jack Dorsey).

I didn't like being a taxi driver. I was convinced people were talking behind my back.

Don't treat people as dangerous but cover your arse in case they are.

Today is the tomorrow you worried about yesterday and all is well.

Every man dies, but not every man lives.

Your job is to find what's around the next corner.

Anyone who has never made a wrong turning has never tried anything.

No journey is ever finished.

You miss 100% of the shots you don't take.

The nail that sticks out gets hammered.

If you win the rat race you're still a rat.

If you want to discover new oceans you must be brave enough to lose sight of the shore.

You are not just responsible for the things you do, you are responsible for the things you don't do.

Your eyes on the stars and your feet on the ground.

You only appreciate the highest mountain if you've been in the deepest valley.

Cream always rises to the top but it also goes off.

Attitudes are contagious, so be careful of yours.

A paragraph should be like a ladies skirt – long enough to cover the essentials but short enough to keep it interesting.

Knowledge is knowing a tomato is a fruit, wisdom is knowing not to put it in a fruit salad.

I did have this woman once, she said 'I've got no money, can I work it off?' It was a bit sad really, she was well past her sell-by date, I said 'No love, have it on me'.

Never plant a cherry stone and expect an apple tree.

People who live in glass houses should never undress.

Just because you're paranoid it doesn't mean that they're not out to get you.

In New York City, a lot of people think 'the great outdoors' is the area between your front door and a taxi cab.

Life is like a set of stairs, if you look back you will trip.

In life big things become small, small things become big.

Do one-legged dusks swim in circles? [response to a silly question]

All foxes grow old, not all grow grey.

Keep trying to get to the top of the ladder, just make sure the ladder is leaning against the right wall.

No good deed goes unpunished.

If you can't be brilliant be useful.

We can't always build a future for our youth but we can build our youth for the future.

Calling a taxi in Texas is like calling for a rabbi in Iraq.

Was I always going to be here? No I was not. I was going to be homeless at one time, a taxi driver, truck driver, or any kind of job that would get me a crust of bread. You never know what's going to happen.

What did the taxi driver say to the wolf who got into his cab? 'Where wolf?'

I shared a London taxi with a group of spotty youths. They thought it was an acne carriage.

A taxi driver sees two bags of crisps strolling along the side of the road. He stops and asks if they need a lift. They say 'No thanks, we're Walkers'.

THE THREE TREES. BLETCHLEY.

The Three Trees public house, Far Bletchley. Ref: Chap 3, p31.
Courtesy of the Essam Postcard Collection, Living Archive, Milton Keynes

Appendix 3: Travelling from, travelling on ...

This study is not just about taxi drivers in Milton Keynes at a certain period of time, it builds on, and relates to, research and understanding across a range of wider topics. As well, then, as the lives and culture of taxi drivers (as yet, as I suggest in Chapter 1, rather little studied) and the ethnography of Milton Keynes, these include the following – just a succinct list, further elaboration will be easy for those working in these areas:

- Cultural and urban anthropology and folklore
- History and culture of hired transport
- The local economy
- Freelance workers
- Immigration, incorporation and social mobility
- Concepts and practices around 'place'
- Multiculturalism
- Transport and town planning
- Gift exchange
- Story and narrative '
- Popular wisdom
- Knowledge, mind, and memory processes
- Local religious and moral concepts and practices
- Names and naming practices
- Personal identity and its conceptualisation
- Life stories and their role

The methodology and subject matter of anthropology, especially auto-ethnography and 'anthropology at home'.

Hopefully the account here will in turn encourage, and form a foundation for, further critical studies on these topics.

Acknowledgements

Very many thanks to Hastings Donnan, Caroline Humphrey, Jo O'Driscoll (MK Taxi Licensing) and the many taxi drivers who so kindly shared some of their experiences with me.

Also, for the illustrations, special thanks for various images to Garner and Stokoe 2000, Ingram 1977, Lahiri-Dutt and Williams 2010, Munro 2014, Townsend 2009 and others noted in the text; to the individual taxi drivers who graciously allowed me to photograph them and their vehicles; and to the most generous photographers in the world, those of unsplash and pixabay.

A particular thank you to Usman Khan, who designed and created the front and back covers.

Also to cartographer and editor John Hunt for his layout, design and publishing coordination (www.mapperou.com).

Overall I am immeasurably grateful to the taxi drivers who have so generously shared their knowledge and insights, and opened up new worlds, cross-cultural and other, for me in the dream-like spaces of their cabs.

Select references (Note: within text and footnotes https and www are generally omitted)

https://www.milton-keynes.gov.uk/environmental-health-and-trading-standards/licensing/hackney-carriage-private-hire/.
https://www.milton-keynes.gov.uk/assets/attach/63284/Guide-for-New-Taxi-Drivers-2020.pdf/.
https://en.wikipedia.org/wiki/Cultural_memory/.
https://en.wikipedia.org/wiki/Collective_memory/.

Anderson, William (1990) *Green Man: the archetype of our oneness with the earth*, Harper, 1990.
Anon (2013) *How 2 become a London taxi driver*, How2become Ltd.
Anon (2014) 'Skilled migrants drive taxis to survive', http://e2nz.org/migrant-stories/chapter-2/skilled-migrants-drive-taxis-to-survive/.
Anon (2022) Autoethnography', *Wikipedia*, https://en.wikipedia.org/wiki/Autoethnography.
Assmann, J. (2008). 'Communicative and cultural memory', in A. Erll & A. Nünning (eds), *Cultural Memory Studies. An International and Interdisciplinary Handbook*, Berlin.
Bartlett, Frederick (1932) *Remembering: A Study in Experimental and Social Psychology*, Cambridge University Press.
Billet, Marion (2012) *Whizzy Wheels: My First London Taxi*, board book, Campbell Books.
Bochner, Arthur (2016) *Evocative Autoethography: Writing Lives and Telling Stories*, Routledge.
Carruthers, Mary (1990/2008) *The Book of Memory: A Study of Memory in Medieval Culture*, Cambridge University Press.
Clyde, Jack (2004) *Glasgow Taxi*, Shepheard PressCoffey, Amanda Jane (1999) *The Ethnographic Self: Fieldwork and the Representation of Identity*, Sage.
Cohen, Sara (2012) 'Live music and urban landscape', *Social Semiotics* 22/3: 587-603.
Connerton, Paul (1989) *How Societies Remember*, Cambridge University Press.
Davies, Charlotte Aull (2008) *Reflexive Ethnography, A Guide to Researching Selves and Others*, Routledge.
Donnan, Hastings (2015) Personal communication.
Eales, William (c2005) *London Taxis at War*, The Author.
Findlay, Douglas J. (2010) *Taxi! Never a dull day: a cabbie remembers*, Berlinner.
Finnegan, Ruth (1989/2007) *The Hidden Musicians. Music making in an English town*, Cambridge University Press / Wesleyan University Press.
Finnegan, Ruth (1998/2019) *Tales of the City*, Cambridge University Press / Callender Press.
Finnegan, Ruth (2005) *Participating in the Knowledge Society: researchers beyond the university walls*, Palgrave-Macmillan.
Finnegan, Ruth (ed,) (2017a) *Entrancement: The Consciousness of Dreaming, Music and the World*, University of Wales Press.
Finnegan, Ruth (2017b) 'The power of names', Utley Memorial Lecture, American Folklore Society, unpublished.
Finnegan, Ruth (2020) *The Hidden Ordinary*, Callender Press.
Finnegan, Ruth (2021) *Taxi Drivers, The Hidden Subject*, Callender Press.
Forrest, John (2022) *Doing Field Projects: Methods and Practice for Social and Anthropological Research*, Wiley-Blackwell.
Gambetta, Diego and Heather Hamill (2005) Streetwise: *How Taxi Drivers Establish Customers' Trustworthiness*, New York, Sage.
Garner, Simon and Stokoe, Giles (2000) *Taxi!* Frances Lincoln.

Gates, Graham (comp) (2011) *London Taxi Driver Slang*, Abson Books.

Geertz, Clifford (1983) *Local Knowledge*, New York: Basic Books.

Genova, Lisa (2021) *Remember: The Science of Memory and the Art of Forgetting*, Harmony.

Gilbey, Walter (1903/2019), *Early Carriages and Roads*, Wentworth Press.

Hallsworth, Simon (2009) *Street Crime*, Routledge.

Henry, Lee (2012) *Belfast Taxi. A drive through history, one fare at a time*, Blackstaff Press.

Ingram, Arthur (1977) *Horse-drawn Vehicles since 1760*, Blandford Press.

Kidron, Carol (2016) 'Memory', https://www.oxfordbibliographies.com/view/document/obo-9780199766567/obo-9780199766567-0155.xml/.

Lahiri-Dutt, Kuntala, and David Williams (2010) *Moving Pictures. Rickshaw art of Bangladesh*, Mapin Publishing.

Lawuyi, O,B. (1988) 'The world of the Yoruba taxi driver. An interpretative approach to vehicle slogans', *Africa* 58: 1-12.

Lockett, John (2017) *Diary of a Taxi Driver*, Brown Dogs Books and The Self-Publishing Partnership.

McGowan, Fiona and Donnan, Hastings (2007) 'Sensing risk: driver-walker and walker-driver interaction in the city', ESRC End of a Grant Report.

Majevadia, Jamiesha (ed) (2016) *Where We Live Now: perspectives on place and policy*, British Academy.

Mathew, Biju (2005) *Taxi! Cabs and capitalism in New York City*, ILR Press.

Mauss, Marcel (1925) Essai sur le don, in *L'Année Sociologique*, English translation by Guyer, Jane (2016), HAU.

Miller, Danny (2004) (ed.) *Car Cultures*, Berg.

Milton Keyes Development Corporation/MKDC (1967-) *Reports*, MKDC.

Moran, Joe (2006) *On Roads. A hidden history*, Profile Books.

Munro, Bill (2009) *Taxi Jubilee. Fifty years of the Austin FX4 London taxi*, Earlswood Press.

Munro, Bill (2014) *London Taxis. A full history*, Earlswood Press.

Murphy, Fiona (2014) *Integration in Ireland: the everyday lives of African migrants*, Manchester University Press.

Murrer, Sally (2021) 'Hundreds fewer taxis and private hire vehicles in Milton Keynes', *MKCitizen*, 10 August.

Nelson, Katie (2020) 'Doing fieldwork, methods in cultural anthropology', https://perspectives.pressbooks.com/chapter/doing-fieldwork-methods-in-cultural-anthropology/

O'Driscoll, Jo (2022) Personal communication.

Parry, Philip and Pye, Glenn (2012) *Taxi Tales*, The Authors.

Salomon, Eugene (2013) *Confessions of a New York Taxi Driver*, The Friday Project.

Shabaya, John (2020) From Mud Hut to Cambridge, An incredible journey, Balestier Press.

Smith, D. J. (1994) *Discovering Horse-drawn Vehicles*, Shire Publications.

Solomon, Mark (2011) *Black Cab Wisdom*, Summersdale Publishers.

Thomson, Alistair (2006) (ed) *The Oral History Reader*, Routledge.

Thrift, Nigel (2001) 'Driving in the city', *Theory, Culture and Society* 21, 4/5: 41-59.

Townsend, Alf (2007) *The London Cabbie, a life's knowledge*, The History Press.

Townsend, Alf (2009) *The Black Cab Story*, The History Press.

Urry, J. (2002) 'Mobility and proximity', *Sociology* 36: 255-74.

Vergunst, Jo Lee and Ingold, Tim (eds) (2016) *Ways of Walking: Ethnography and Practice on Foot*, –Routledge.

Lightning Source UK Ltd.
Milton Keynes UK
UKHW050153071122
411748UK00001B/1

9 781739 893767